MONUMENTAL INSCRIPTIONS

URQUHART OLD

Parish of Urquhart

Moray

Compiled by
**Members of the Moray and Banff Branch of the ANESFHS
and the Moray Burial Ground Research Group**

Edited by
Helen Mitchell FSA Scot
and
Bruce B. Bishop FSA Scot

ISBN 1-900173-95-6
First Published
April 2006

Published by
Aberdeen and North-East Scotland Family History Society

Printed by
Rainbow Enterprises, Howe Moss Crescent, Kirkhill Industrial Estate, Dyce,
Aberdeen

INTRODUCTION

The Old Churchyard of Urquhart is situated just to the south of the village, and was in use as the principal burial ground for the parish until about 1970, when it was replaced by the New Cemetery. The buried tombstones for Urquhart Old Churchyard will be published in volume 4 of "The Forgotten Tombstones of Moray" series later in 2006.

The numbering system has been co-ordinated with the system already in use on the Moray Council LIBINDEX.

The index contains all surnames, even when used as a middle name, as these could indicate the surnames of parents or grandparents. Transcriptions are exactly 'as read', including the use of superscripts and subscripts, and where punctuation is used on the stone this has only been edited where required in order to avoid misinterpretation.

ACKNOWLEDGEMENTS

The Society wishes to thank all concerned in the preparation of this index. The recording at Urquhart Old Churchyard was carried out by members of both the Moray and Banff Branch of the Aberdeen and North East Scotland Family History Society and the Moray Burial Ground Research Group. The history of the site, indexing and graveyard plans are the work of Bruce Bishop, the editing has been carried out by Helen Mitchell and Bruce Bishop, and Keith Mitchell has compiled a photographic archive of the tombstones.

Thanks are due to Jean Shirer and Edna Cromarty for their comments and editing of the original draft of this booklet.

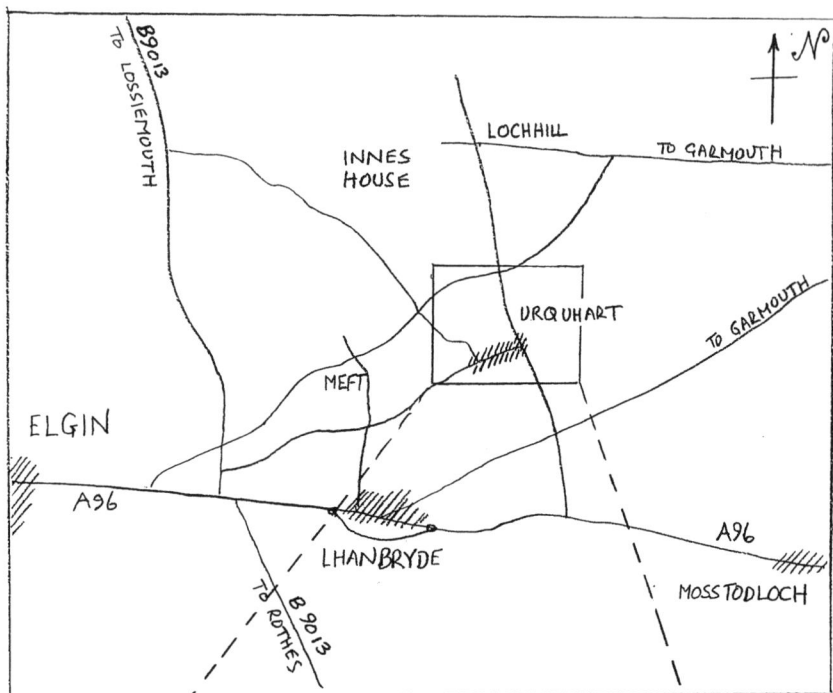

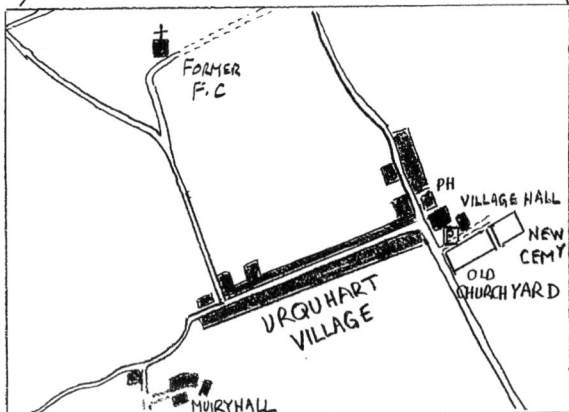

Location of the Burial Ground

CONTENTS

A brief history of the Old Churchyard of Urquhart

The Priory of Urquhart was founded by King David I in about 1125 in honour of the Blessed Trinity, and was a cell of the Benedictine Abbey of Dunfermline. It was incorporated into the Priory of Pluscarden in 1453 by a Papal Bull issued by Pope Nicolas V, and no trace now remains of the priory, which was situated at a site now known as the 'Abbey Well'. A carved wheel-cross built into the church hall is the only surviving relic of the priory, and no associated burial ground has been traced.

The general population of the parish, however, made use of the parish church which was situated near to the centre of the old churchyard. This church had been in existence for a long time, in fact in a deed of 1237 it is indicated that the church at Urquhart had *"past memory of man"* supplied divine service and the holy sacraments to the *"inhabitants of Meft, Sallelcot, Byn and Garmauch"*. Garmouth was at various times in its history part of the parish of Urqhart, at other times part of Essil or Speymouth parish.

In 1350 it is recorded that the church of Urquhart was taxed at 60 merks, a higher rate than many of the other small parish churches, indicating that it was of some importance to the Bishops of Moray. On 10th June 1454, during the removal of the priory of Urquhart to Pluscarden, transumpts of two charters were signed in the parish church of Urquhart by *"John of Bonale, Prior of Urquhart, Bartholemew a monk, and John, son of Alan, a priest"*.

The first post-Reformation mention of the church is in November 1567 when Robert Keyth was the minister of the united parishes of Urquhart, 'Lambride' and Essil. John Blundshell was reader at that time. Patrick Balfour became minister in 1574, and by 1576 Alexander Sinclair held the position. In 1580 Urquhart became a separate charge under John Innes.

Urquhart was erected into a Burgh of Barony, and then a Burgh of Regality, and by 1571 it was referred to in various charters as the *"Barrony and Regality of Vrquhart"*. This allowed the Laird at the House of Innes to dispense justice locally, except in cases of murder or treason, and the punishments often seemed to depend on the mood of the *"Barron Court"* at the time. The church which had served the parish from earliest times was demolished in 1655, and services were held in the hall at Innes House until the opening of the new church in late 1658.

The Urquhart Kirk Session Minutes for most of the 17th and 18th centuries have not survived, but the church, together with the neighbouring school and inn, were the centre of life for the parish throughout these years. The Disruption of 1843 resulted in the building of the Free Church, but all of the burials in the parish continued to take place in the old churchyard.

MONUMENTAL INSCRIPTIONS

URQUHART CHURCHYARD

URQUHART PARISH, MORAY

1. In memory of ELIZABETH COOK beloved wife of WILLIAM LAING, Farmer, Wallfield, who died 25TH July 1896, aged 54 years. Also JOHN who died in infancy. Also of the said WILLIAM LAING, who died at Wallfield, 6TH January 1913, aged 66 years. Also their son ALEXANDER who was killed in France on 16TH August 1916, aged 32 years. Also of their daughter ELIZABETH who died 12TH August 1953 aged 74 years.

2. In loving memory of WILLIAM LAING, Farmer, who died at Wallfield 14TH Nov. 1941, aged 68 years. Also his wife JESSIE REID who died 6TH March 1944 aged 65 years. Also their son WILLIAM REID LAING, Farmer, Wallfield who died 27TH Feb. 1978 aged 67 years.

3a. In loving memory of JANET GILLAN, wife of Rev. JAMES MORRISON, Minister at Urquhart, born 28TH May 1827, died 26TH April 1893. Also of his daughter CATHERINE FRASER, born 19TH May 1862 died 8TH September 1914. And of their eldest daughter BEATRICE HOYES born 27TH October 1849 died 27TH November 1927.
    "More then conquerors through him that loved us." Rom. VIII. 37.

3b. In loving memory of the Rev. JAMES MORRISON, Minister of the Free Church of Scotland at Urquhart, 1844 – 1899. Born at Auldearn 30TH May, 1816, died at Elgin 1ST January 1899.
    "His servants shall serve him and they shall see his face." REV. XXII. 3&4.

3c. In loving memory of ROBINA, youngest daughter of the Rev. JAMES MORRISON, who died at the Manse of Urquhart, 27TH April 1884, aged 25. And of his son ALEXANDER HOYES who died 28TH February 1851, aged four months. "There remaineth therefore a rest for the people of God." Hebrews IV. 9.

4. In loving memory of JAMES CANT late Farmer of Speyslaw who died at Crosshill, Garmouth 8TH of August 1896 in the 83RD year of his age. Also his wife MARJORY NORVAL who died 17TH June 1929 aged 95 years.

4a. *Heart shaped stone.*
    NELLIE.

4b. *Mason's Block.*
    A. N.

4c. NEWLANDS. Dear grandparents JAMES died 1931, MARGARET died 1944 and MARGARET JANE died 1978. A dearly loved daughter & aunt.

4d.   *Mason's Block.*
      (*Illegible.*)

5.   Erected by AGNES REID, in loving memory of her parents ANDREW REID, died 25TH Decr. 1899, aged 61 years. JANE ANDERSON, died 9TH June 1883, aged 33 years. Also her brothers, ANDREW, died 22ND Decr. 1897, aged 22 years. WILLIAM, died 13TH Novr. 1899, aged 21 years. JAMES, who died at New-Elgin 18TH Octr. 1906, aged 34 years. Also her sisters ANNIE who died at The Royal Infirmary, Aberdeen 15TH Decr. 1909, aged 20. JANE who died 9TH Jany. 1903, aged 29 years. The above AGNES REID, died at Urquhart Village, 2ND Augt. 1928 aged 48 years.
      "Gone but not forgotten."

6.   Erected by ANNIE REID in loving memory of her father ANDREW REID, Farmer, Maverston who died 14TH October 1885 in the 77TH year of his age. Also her mother, JANE HARDIE who died 12TH Novr. 1857 in the 89TH year of her age. And the said ANNIE REID who died at Forres 30TH Sep^t. 1925 in the 86TH year of her age.
      "Gone but not forgotten."

7.   In loving memory of JAMES REID, Farmer, Maverston, who died 17TH July 1911, aged 76 years. And his son WILLIAM, who died 22ND October 1890, aged 26 years. Also his daughter JANE, who died 1ST May 1895, aged 29 years. Also his wife AGNES MILNE who died at Maverston 3RD September 1935 aged 90 years. Also their son JAMES who died in South Africa 3RD September 1961 aged 84 years.

8.   In memory of JAMES MURRAY who died in Elgin in 1850, aged 64 & his spouse ISABELLA CANT who died at Woodside Croft, Urquhart 10 April 1862, aged 76, of their family JAMES died 20 Jany. 1875, aged 65 & ISABELLA on 9 Augt. 1904, aged 86. MARGARET MURRAY died June 6TH 1914, aged 88 years. WILLIAM MURRAY died March 1ST 1918 aged 66 years.

9.   MURDO MACKENZIE died at Maverston, Urquhart, 6TH November 1893, aged 63. "His life was stormy may he rest in peace" Also his wife MARGARET M^{AC}GREGOR who died at Elgin 15TH May 1903 aged 71. Their grandson MURDO M^{AC}KENZIE died 12TH Sep. 1922 aged 24. And their only daughter ANN MACKENZIE died 21ST March 1932 aged 82.

9a.   In memoriam ANNIE MACKENZIE.

9b.   *Mason's Block.*
      (*Illegible.*)

10.   Erected by MARGARET WATSON, New-Elgin in affectionate remembrance of her dearly beloved husband, GEORGE SIMPSON, born 9TH August 1855, died 24TH January 1900. And of their children ALEXANDER, born 21ST February 1882 died 27TH February 1896. MARGARET ROBB, MARY-ANN, & PETER, who died in infancy. Also of the said MARGARET WATSON who died 18TH April 1947 aged 90 years. Also their

son GEORGE SIMPSON, J.P. late Sub-Postmaster, Hopeman who died 1ST August 1954 aged 69 years. Also their great grandchild HARRY K.S. SHIACH, born London, Ontario, 11-1-57 (*11th January 1957*), died Dundee, Scotland, 19-1-58 (*19th January 1958.*)
"The morning cometh." ISA. 21. 12.
(*Mason, W.T. Hendry, Elgin.*)

11. In ever loving memory of GEORGE SIMPSON who died at Muirton Lossiemouth 1ST August 1954 aged 70 years and his beloved wife ANNABELLA SIMPSON who died 10TH January 1957 aged 68 years. Rest-in-peace.

11a. *Mason's Block.*
A. S.

12. Erected to the memory of MARGARET FOTHERINGHAM wife of WILLIAM DUNCAN died 2ND Dec. 1947 aged 58 years. Also her sons, ROBERT died in infancy. Also JAMES 2ND Seaforths, killed in action in N.W. Europe on 4TH Nov. 1944 aged 26 years, buried Berger-op-zoom, Holland. Also GEORGE died 23RD June 1967 aged 45 years, cremated at Oakworth, Yorkshire. Also her husband WILLIAM DUNCAN died 9TH Jan. 1970 aged 86 years. Also ISOBEL (TIBBY) died 9TH Dec. 1979. Also JOHN (JOCK) died 17TH May 1989. Also ANNIE (NAN) died 28TH Dec. 1997.

12a. *Mason's Block.*
W. D.

12b. *Mason's Block.*
W. D.

13a. *Mason's Block.*
J. W.

13. Sacred to the memory of ALEXANDER WILLIAMSON, Mason, Blackdam, who died 6TH June, 1890 aged 56 years. Also of his wife ELSPET SANDESON, who died at Blackdam 27TH December 1872 aged 84 years. This stone is placed here in grateful remembrance by their grandaughter ELSPET TAYLOR, Pensylvania, (*sic*) U. S. America. Also ALEXANDER WILLIAMSON their grandson who died at Albany on 30TH July 1876 aged 23 years and JEAN GORDON their grandaughter who died at Lochee on the 22ND Oct. 1878 aged 21(?) years and interred in the Lochee Cemetery, Dundee.

14. In loving memory of our mother ISABELLA WILLIAMSON died at Urquhart 3RD Oct. 1891 aged 26 years. And our father JAMES MITCHELL DUNCAN who died 15TH May 1921 aged 64 years. Also their daughter ANN died 4TH Nov. 1964 aged 74 years and their son ALEXANDER WILLIAMSON died 13TH May 1974 aged 82 years.

15. 1889. Erected by JOHN WILLIAMSON, Lochs, in memory of his wife JANE ALEXANDER who died there 10TH September 1884, aged 73 years. Also their daughter ELSPET WILLIAMSON who died at Lochhill 3RD July 1870, aged 26 years. Also the said JOHN WILLIAMSON who died at Lochs, Urquhart 15TH Novr. 1890 aged 76 years. And his son JOHN who died 14TH March 1911, aged 72 years.

16. Erected to the memory of WILLIAM JUNNER, who died at Inverness 13TH Novr. 1876, aged 27 years and interred here. Also his wife JEAN WILLIAMSON who died at Muir-of-Urquhart 4TH May 1929 aged 82 years.

16a. *Mason's Block.*
IV II(?).

17. 1867. Erected by JOHN MUNRO, Miller, Burnie Stripe Mills in memory of his daughter ANN MUNRO who died 28TH April 1867 aged 22 years. Also of the said JOHN MUNRO, who died 1ST May 1883 in the 77TH year of his age. And of his wife JANE GORDON who died 26TH April 1897 in the 80TH year of her age.

18. In loving memory of our dear parents ANNIE CALDER beloved wife of JOHN MUNRO died 16TH Sept. 1962 aged 74 years. Also the said JOHN MUNRO died 30TH Aug. 1964 aged 84 years of Bruiach Mills, Kiltarlity & Burniestripe Mills, Garmouth. Erected by their sons.

18a. *Mason's Block.*
MUNRO 1867.

19. In loving memory of ROBINA, youngest daughter of JOHN HENDERSON, Engineer, who died at Hull 23RD February 1899 aged 21 years. Also JAMES HENDERSON, Marine Engineer, who died at Colon, Colombia, 22ND July 1901, aged 30 years. Also the above JOHN HENDERSON, Engineer, who died at Don Cottage, Mosstodloch, Fochabers 27TH Octr. 1918 aged 78 years, and of his wife MARGARET CRAMOND who also died there 20TH January 1928, aged 86 years. Also MARGARET HENDERSON died 4TH November 1955, aged 86 years. And his daughter MARY HENDERSON died 29TH March 1963 aged 89 years.

20. Sacred to the memory of ANNIE SUTHERLAND born at Windyhillock, Boharm, Nov. 1836, died June 1892 and her husband ANGUS MACDONALD, born at Duthil, Feb. 1832, died Aug. 1916 and their daughter JESSIE ANN born May 1866, died April 1891, and their son JAMES born 1862, died Nov. 1915, also their son ANGUS born 1872, died Dec. 1929.

21. 1884. Sacred to the memory of JAMES CAMPBELL, Farmer, Newfield, who died 10TH April 1864 aged 74 years, and ELIZABETH MACGREGOR, his wife, who died at Newfield, 31ST March 1883, aged 83 years. Also of ALEXANDER CAMPBELL, lost in the "City of Dunedin", New Zealand Waters, May 1865.

"Rest in the Lord and wait patiently for him."

22. In loving memory of our dear parents WILLIAM G. McLENNAN who died 23rd August 1971 aged 71 years, beloved husband of LILLY McLENNAN who died 22nd December 1993 aged 70 years, dear mum and dad of BILLY, GRACE, KATHLEEN and RICHARD. "Requiescant in Pace."

23. Erected by DAVID GREGOR, in memory of his father JAMES GREGOR, who died the 20 September 1824 and of his brother, JAMES who died the 16th July 1822.

24. In loving memory of WILLIAM NEWLANDS, Sunnybrae, Inchberry, beloved husband of JANE MORRISON, who died 31 July 1920 aged 76 years. The said JANE MORRISON died 23 Jan. 1938 aged 88.

25. Erected by HUGH HOOD, Clattrenbrigs (sic), in memory of his wife SARAH SIMON, who died there 31ST March 1883, aged 75 years. And of their son WILLIAM who died 18TH December 1853, aged 14 years. Also of the said HUGH HOOD, who died 22ND November 1890, aged 87 years. Also of their son HUGH who died 9TH April 1898, aged 60 years. Also of their grandson WILLIAM HOOD M[c]ADAM, who died 10TH April 1898, aged 28 years. Also their daughter SARAH HOOD, who died 30TH Jan. 1932, aged 82 years.

26. 1879. Erected by HELEN SIEVWRIGHT in memory of her mother, ISABELLA HOOD, who died at Clatternbrigs (sic) on the 18TH December 1878, aged 73 years. Also the said HELEN SIEVWRIGHT, who died at Elgin, 18TH January 1907, aged 77 years.

27. Erected to the memory of HUGH HOOD, Farmer, who died at Easter Lochs, Garmouth, 4TH December 1914. aged 75 years. Also his son GEORGE who died 27TH Nov. 1920, aged 34 years, interred at Kildrummy Churchyard. Also JESSIE MILTON wife of the said HUGH HOOD who died at Easter Lochs, 15TH May 1929, aged 80 years. Also his son WILLIAM MUIL HOOD who died at Dunkirk, Garmouth 31ST Dec. 1947 aged 74 years. Also his son HUGH HOOD retired Farmer, Dunkirk, Garmouth who died 2ND May 1954 aged 78 years. Also his son JOHN HOOD who died in British Colombia 26TH May 1955 aged 74 years.
(*Mason, Wilson, Elgin.*)

28. Erected by JOHN HOOD, in memory of his daughter MARGARET, who died at Garmouth, 9TH Feb[y]. 1899 aged 13 years, and of his daughter JEANNIE who died at Fochabers 11TH Sep[r]. 1899, aged 20 years. Also the said JOHN HOOD who died at Fochabers 1ST June 1918, aged 76 years. Also his wife JANE LOGIE who died at Fochabers 13TH Dec[r]. 1933, aged 88 years. And of their daughter ANNIE who died at Fochabers, on 26TH April 1961.
(*Mason, Goodwillie & Son.*)

28a. *Mason's Block.*

J. HOOD.

28b. *Mason's Block.*
J. HOOD.

29. In loving memory of GEORGE WATSON who died at Rose Cottage, Urquhart, 24TH Decr. 1918 aged 69 years. Also his sons GODFREY who died 27TH Jany. 1899, aged 20 years. ROBERT ALEX^R who died at Aberlour 2ND April 1914 aged 39 years, and is interred there. CHRISTINA M. WATSON sister of the above GEORGE WATSON who died 11TH April 1929 aged 74 years. Also of his wife ANN REID who died at Rose Cottage 28TH Sep^t. 1932 aged 90 years. Also their youngest daughter MARY (POLLY) MACKENZIE who died at Rose Cottage, Urquhart 9TH July 1955 beloved wife of ALEX MURDOCH. "I know that my redeemer liveth."

29a. In loving memory of GODFREY WATSON aged 20 years.

30. Erected by JOHN M^{c}KINZIE, Shoemaker, in memory of his father, JOHN M^{c}KINZIE who died 26th May 1830 aged 24 years. Also his spouse ISABELLA CHALMERS who died 13th Feby. 1849 aged 51 years. Also the said JOHN M^{c}KINZIE who died at Glasgow 22nd April 1849 aged 19 years.

31. *Heart shaped plaque.*
In loving memory of MARGARET DOCKAR died 26TH Feby 1910 aged 25.

32. 1889. Erected by JAMES HARDIE, in memory of his wife JESSIE WILLIAMSON, who died at Fochabers 20TH August 1888, aged 34 years.

33. *Heart shaped plaque.*
(Blank.)

34. In loving memory of ALEXANDER M^{c}KENZIE who died at Lochs Cottage, Urquhart 2ND Jany. 1913, aged 78 years. Also his son JOHN who died 14TH Jany. 1869, aged 11 years, and his son in law JOHN REID who died 26TH Jany. 1890, aged 24 years. Also ISABELLA WILLIAMSON wife of the above ALEXANDER M^{c}KENZIE who died at Lochs Cottage, Urquhart 13TH Decr. 1924, aged 88 years. And their daughters, JESSIE wife of ALEX. MARR who died 19TH Jan. 1915 aged 47. JANE ANN widow of JOHN REID who died 5TH March 1936 aged 71. And their daughter ISABELLA who died 31ST Decr. 1967 aged 81, widow of JAMES MACKIE, lost at sea 1922.
Erected by his widow and family.

35. Erected by JANE MURDOCH in loving memory of her husband ALEXANDER WILLIAMSON who died at Fife Cottage, Meft, 19TH March 1948 aged 74 years, also the above JANE MURDOCH who died at Elgin 6TH January 1955 aged 86 years. Also their daughter NELLIE WILLOX died in Australia 5TH May 1978 aged 77 years.

35a. In memory of our dear father, from NELLIE, INA and Mother.

35b.   *Book plaque.*
In loving memory of our dear father and mother, from the family.

36.   1901.   Erected by WILLIAM WILLIAMSON in memory of his father JAMES WILLIAMSON, who died at Maverstone, 4TH May 1895, aged 54 years. And his mother, MARGARET MCKAY, who died at Urquhart Village, 4TH March 1910 aged 66 years. Also their youngest daughter CHRISTINA who died at 33 Springbank Terrace, Aberdeen, 9TH Nov. 1941 aged 58 years.

37.   JOHN SHAND, Lochhill, died 1899, his wife ANN HOSSACK died 1911.

37a.   Sacred to the memory of ISABELLA daughter of the late ROBERT GILLAN who died at Elgin 4TH Dec. 1922 aged 70 years.

37b.   *Mason's Block.*
(*Illegible.*)

38.   Erected by JANE THOMPSON in memory of her husband ALEXANDER GILLAN, who died at Urquhart 18th Dec.1858 aged 59 years. Also of the said JANE THOMPSON who died 12th November 1880, aged 79 years. And of their son JOHN GILLAN who died at Urquhart 22 April 1905, aged 70 years. And his daughter ISABELLA, died in infancy. Also his wife JANE SINCLAIR, who died 29th December 1948, aged 92 years.

38a.   *Flower holder.*
Fondest memories of my dear mother FREDA.

39.   Sacred to the memory of WILLIAM GILLAN, Shoemaker, Urquhart, who died 17TH May 1887 aged 63 years. And of his daughter MARGARET, who died on Christmas Day 1890. Also of his son JAMES, who died in infancy. Also of JANE MILNE, wife of the said WILLIAM GILLAN who died at Urquhart 18TH June 1909, aged 79 years, and of his son GEORGE who died 18TH Decr. 1913. Also of their son WILLIAM, who died 12TH July 1914. And of their son JOHN, who died 11TH Nov. 1939 aged 68 years.
In memory of ROBERT GILLAN, died 15TH May 1951, buried at East Lands, Galashiels.

40.   Sacred to the memory of ALEXANDER GILLAN, Merchant, who died at Maida, Elgin, 16TH March 1936 aged 80 years. And ANN STUART, his wife who also died at Maida 21ST May 1937 aged 77 years. ANNIE DUNCAN GILLAN their eldest daughter died at Maida, Elgin 9TH January 1948 aged 64 years.
(*Mason, L. Morrell.*)

41.   In memory of HUGH FLETCHER, born at Littletown in the Parish of Croy, Nairnshire, on 14TH August 1778, died at Garmouth on 22ND June 1866. And of MARGARET THOMSON his spouse, born 12TH September 1788 died 17TH January 1870. Also of two of their children JOHN ROSE FLETCHER

and ÆNEAS THOMSON FLETCHER. And of ISOBEL THOMSON sister of the said MARGARET THOMSON who died 24TH September 1881.

41a. *Mason's Block.*
     A. E.

42. Erected by the children & grandchildren of PETER BAIN who died at Urquhart 4TH August 1908 aged 83 years, also his wife JANE GRIGOR who died 23RD August 1908 aged 81 years. Also their sons ROBERT JOHN who died 7TH August 1869 aged 4 years. PETER died 25TH July 1877 aged 15 years. Also their daughter JESSIE who died in U.S.A. 30TH June 1890 aged 38 years. And their grand-daughter JEANNIE G. DUFFUS, Music-teacher, Elgin, died 11TH June 1931, aged 44 years. Also their daughter HANNAH BAIN or DUFFUS died 22ND March 1943, aged 79 years. Her husband JAMES ANGUS DUFFUS, died 13TH Dec. 1942 aged 81 years.

42a. JEANNIE.

43. In loving memory of CONSTANCE LESLIE, D.A. who was accidentally killed 14TH Jan. 1935 aged 24 years.

44. In loving memory of ALEXANDER ROBERTSON, who died at Redbog, 23RD Decr. 1905, aged 74 years. Also of his son ALEXANDER H. ROBERTSON, who died at New-York, U.S.A. 30TH April 1897, aged 35 years. Also his grandson JACK ROBERTSON killed in action on the Marne, France, 20TH July 1918 aged 25 years. Also his son JAMES F. ROBERTSON who died at Redbog 30TH March 1921 aged 45 years. Also his wife JESSIE HOOD who died at Redbog, 19TH May 1929 aged 92 years.
    Erected by his widow & family.

45. Erected by ALEXANDER HOOD, Farmer, Redbog, to the memory of his spouse, JANNET KNIGHT, who died, 25TH Octr. 1848 aged 45 years. Also his son HUGH who died, 5TH May 1849 aged 14 years. Both greatly regreted (*sic*). Also of the said ALEXANDER HOOD, who died at Redbog 24TH March 1882, aged 82 years.

46. In loving memory of JOHN HOOD ROBERTSON who died at Cranloch, 6TH Dec. 1927, aged 58 years. Also his daughter ANNIE M^{c}KENZIE who died at Bournemouth 9TH Feb. 1929, aged 28 years. Also his beloved wife MARGARET WALKER who died at Moss-side 20TH August 1959, aged 85 years.
    Flower holder. R.

47. Erected to the memory of HUGH HOOD, Farmer, Redbogg (*sic*), who died 18TH December 1843 aged 75 years, also his beloved spouse MARGARET BARREN who died 19TH January 1857, aged 86 years.
    Erected by his famely (*sic*).

48. Erected by HUGH J. HOOD, in memory of his father, JOHN HOOD, Chief Engineer, R.N., who died at Red-bog, S^t. Andrews, on the 19TH January 1870, aged 57 years.
(*Mason, T. Goodwillie.*)

48a. *Plaque.*
In loving memory Mother dear.

49. 1923. Erected by JEANNIE SHAND in memory of her husband ALEXANDER HOOD who died 20. May 1923 aged 75 years. Also the said JEANNIE SHAND who died 23. May 1938 aged 83 years.
(*Mason, J.S. Morren, Elgin.*)

50. In memory of JOHN ALLAN and his wife JESSIE HOOD of Muiryhall, also their two sons who both died in infancy.
(*Mason, J. Robertson & Son, Hardgate, Aberdeen.*)

51. In memoriam. ANDREW M^{c}KENZIE died at Lossiemouth 22nd Feb. 1899 aged 73. His wife JANE SCOTT died at Nether Meft 26th Dec. 1909 aged 82. Their son WILLIAM died 3rd Jan. 1914 aged 57. MAGGIE LIZZIE, died at Lossiemouth, 17TH Oct. 1900 aged 11. GORDON died 11TH Feb. 1895 aged 4mths, daughter and son of ANDREW M^{c}KENZIE, Jr. died 4TH Sep.1919 aged 67. His wife MARG^T Y.L. HAY died 17TH Jan. 1944 aged 89. Their daughter JANET J.S. died 16TH Sep. 1937 aged 49. Their daughter GEORGINA died 5TH July 1948 aged 57.

52. Erected by MARGARET ROY in memory of her husband WILLIAM MACKENZIE, Farmer in Maverstown, who died 7th August 1857, aged 73 years. Also her son WILLIAM MACKENZIE who died 11th June 1854, aged 45 years. Also the said MARGARET ROY who died 7TH August 1863 aged 78 years.

53. Erected by his family in memory of ROBERT MACKENZIE who died at Maverston 13TH March 1933 aged 69. And his daughter AMELIA AMY died 5TH Nov. 1925 aged 25. Also his wife JANE ANDERSON died 20TH July 1965 aged 91.

54. 1890. Erected by his sons in memory of GEORGE M^{c}KENZIE, who died at Maverston, 6TH December 1885, aged 70 years. And of his daughter MARGARET, who died 21ST March 1861, aged 20 years. And of his son GEORGE, who died 17TH April 1872, aged 22 years. Also his daughter JESSIE, who died in infancy. Also his wife ISABELLA SUTHERLAND, who died 9TH November 1898 aged 79 years. Also in memory of WILLIAM M^{c}KENZIE, son, who died at Bilston 5TH November 1901, aged 47 years. Also in memory of ALEXANDER H. M^{c}KENZIE, son, who died at Germiston, South Africa, 17TH February 1903, aged 45 years.
"Peace perfect peace."

54a. Erected by P.M. PULLEY to the dear memory of MARGARET JACK who died 6TH Sep^t. 1954 aged 21 years. You're lovely PEGGY JACK you really are, PHIL.

55. Erected by DAVID WISEMAN in loving memory of his wife ISABELLA MILNE who died at Newstynie 22ND Sep^t. 1930 aged 73 years.

56. In memory of WILLIAM HAY, who died at Binns on the 7TH day of March, 1860, aged 72 years, also ISABELLA BRANDER, his wife who died at Hills of Urquhart on the 3RD day of December, 1872, aged 73 years, and of their son, WILLIAM HAY, M.D. who died at Carlisle, on the 5TH day of November, 1879, aged 49 years. Also of their son, Captain JAMES HAY, Commander of the barque Scottish Chief, who was washed over-board and drowned, in the Gulf of Florida, on the morning of the 14TH of April 1881 aged 40 years. Also their daughter MARY HAY died at Elgin 18TH Septr. 1911.

57. Erected by PETER GORDON in loving memory of his son ALEXANDER GORDON who died at Meft 16TH March 1925 aged 35 years.

58. In memory of GEORGE WILLIAMSON beloved husband of JANE MITCHELL who died at Rosehill 2ND Sep. 1925, aged 58 years. Also their son GEORGE who was killed in action in Belgium 4TH Oct. 1917, aged 21 years, also the said JANE MITCHELL who died at Elm Cottage, Urquhart 9TH March 1948 aged 81 years.

58a. *Mason's Block.*
A. S.

58b. *Mason's Block.*
Illegible.

59. In loving memory of ROBERT ELLIS who died at Urquhart 7TH February 1936 aged 72, also of his wife MARGARET GERRIE who died at Urquhart 28TH January 1939 aged 77.
(Mason, Henderson, Elgin.)

60. Erected to the memory of JAMES GERRIE, who died at Lochs of Urquhart, April 8TH 1852, aged 69 years.

60a. *Mason's Block.*
A. C.

60b. *Mason's Block.*
L. BALFOUR.

61. D. Erected by MARY ALLAN in loving memory of her dearly loved husband GEORGE SCOTT DOUGLAS, Farmer, Castlehill, Fochabers, who died on 16TH July 1951. Sadly missed. Also the above MARY ALLAN who died at Castlehill Farm on 7TH Aug. 1970.

(Mason, Wilson, Elgin.)
Flower holder. Happy memories of my dear dad, and mum. JEAN.

62.   Erected by ALEXANDER ELLIS in memory of his wife MARGARET
      FORSYTH who died at Woodside, Blackhills, 12TH Sep^t. 1935 aged 76 years.
      Also of the above ALEXANDER ELLIS who died 2ND Sep^t. 1936 aged 78
      years.
      (Mason, Henderson, Elgin.)

63.   Erected by ALEXANDER ELLIS, in memory of his wife JANE WISEMAN,
      who died at Blackhills, 27TH March 1883 aged 59 years, and their children,
      JANE, died 2ND April 1853. HELLEN, died 30TH April 1855. WILLIAM, died
      25TH April 1869. JESSIE, died 29TH May 1869. Also of the said
      ALEXANDER ELLIS, who died at Woodside, Blackhills, 12TH April 1906,
      aged 83 years.

64.   Erected to the memory of JAMES BOYNE, Farmer, Waterscott, who died
      3RD November 1879 aged 51 years, also his children ANNIE who died 29TH
      June 1869 aged 5 years and two months, CATHERINE SARAH who died
      23RD July 1869 aged 2 years and ten months. WILLIAM who died in infancy.
      Also his wife ANNIE WILLIAMSON who died at Bailiesland, Leuchars 6TH
      December 1916 aged 82 years.

65.   Erected by JOHN & LIZZIE BOYNE in loving memory of their children
      LIZZIE who died 8TH Oct. 1917 aged 26. JAMES aged 2. ANNIE JANE aged
      3. MARGARET HAY aged 2. JAMES ALEX. who died in infancy, also
      JOHN BOYNE who died at Waterscott 20TH July 1944 aged 88 and his wife
      ELIZABETH REID who died 22ND Dec. 1949 aged 94. Also their daughter
      ISABELLA BOYNE who died 17TH Dec. 1963 aged 80. BOYNE.

66.   *Flat Stone.*
      Erected to the memory of JAMES HAY, late Farmer in Waterscott, who died
      21ST May 1799, aged 57 years. And his spouse JANE SHARP who died 12th
      May 1839 aged 83? years, also their son JOHN HAY, Farmer, Waterscott,
      who died there 28th April 1856 aged 73 years.

67.   Erected by ALEXANDER FORSYTH, Farmer in Speyslaw, and his brothers
      – JAMES, WILLIAM, and JOHN, in affectionate remembrance of their
      parents, ISABELLA REID their mother, who died at Speyslaw, 31st July
      1852, aged 69 years. Also, of their father, ALEXANDER FORSYTH, late
      Farmer, Speyslaw, who died 19th April 1853, aged 68 years. Also of the said
      ALEXANDER FORSYTH who died at Urquhart 26TH April 1897 aged 84
      years.

68.   In loving memory of my husband JOHN FORSYTH died 9TH July 1903 aged
      77. Also our infant daughters MARGARET & JAMESINA. Also JANE
      BRANDER his wife, who died at Glasgow 30TH October 1921, aged 94. "In
      thy protecting care," and their daughter WILLIAMINA beloved wife of
      GEO. C. CAMFIELD, died in Glasgow, 28TH Dec. 1945, interred here, also

the above GEORGE CORMACK CAMFIELD beloved husband of WILLIAMINA FORSYTH died in Glasgow 5TH March 1955.

68a. *Mason's Block.*
J. F.

68b. *Mason's Block.*
J. F.

68c. In memory of my uncle A. FORSYTH died April 26 1897 aged 84.

69. JAMES HARDIE died 18TH Oct. 1958 aged 76. WILLIAM ANDREW died 20TH Oct. 1958 aged 74. CHARLES REID died 22ND Mar. 1933 aged 47. Erected by AGNES A.M. FORSYTH.

69a. To the memory of JAMES FORSYTH, Carpenter, Lhanbryde died 17TH June 1938 aged 86. AGNES REID his wife died 3RD Feb. 1926 aged 75. JESSIE GILZEAN died 13TH Mar. 1952 aged 70. Erected by AGNES A.M. FORSYTH.

69b. JOHN AUSTIN died 27TH May 1955 aged 67. ALEXANDER CAMERON died 24TH Nov. 1897 aged 6, and AGNES ANNIE MARGARET FORSYTH died 5TH Nov. 1982 aged 89.
Erected by AGNES A.M. FORSYTH.
(Mason, Henderson.)

69c. *Mason's Block.*
J. F.

69d. *Mason's Block.*
W. DEAN.

70. Erected by JAMES MACDONALD, in memory of his wife JANE DEAN, who died 8th Jany. 1889, aged 42 years.
(Mason, W.T. Hendry, Elgin.)

71. Erected by WILLIAM DEAN, in memory of his wife ISABELLA ANDERSON, who died 23RD Octr. 1894, aged 79 years. Also of the said WILLIAM DEAN, who died 31ST Jany. 1900, aged 79 years.
(Mason, W.T. Hendry, Elgin.)

71a. *Mason's Block.*
W. M.

72. Erected by ISOBEL ANDERSON, Wellhead, Longhill, in memory of her husband ALEXANDER GEDDES who died 11th September 1836 aged 59 years.

73. *Mason's Block.*
W. M^{c}KAY.

74. Erected by ISABELLA M^cKENZIE in memory of her husband JAMES DUNCAN late Farmer in Matthew Mill who died the 19TH day of June 1835 aged 56 years. Also of the above ISABELLA M^cKENZIE, who died at Wards of Garmouth, 16TH Nov. 1861 aged 76 years.

75. Sacred to the memory of JAMES SMITH, who died at Newfield, 3RD Augt. 1887 aged 58 years. Also his wife ELIZABETH LAWRENCE who died at Meft 3RD May 1908, aged 86 years. Also their sons, JOHN who died 24TH March 1874 aged 27 years, and is interred in Birnie Churchyard. WILLIAM, who died 25TH Feby. 1875 aged 11 years. And their mother MARGARET who died 6TH Sep^t. 1900 aged 52 years. Also their youngest daughter ANNIE, who died 12TH March 1929 aged 67 years.

75a. *Mason's Block.*
J. S.

76. In memory of my dear husband JAMES GRAY LEGGE who died 29TH April 1934 aged 55 years. Also his wife ELIZA JANE DOUGLAS who died at Inverness 10TH Aug. 1957 aged 83 years. And their daughter JESSIE ISABELLA, widow of DAVID DAVIDSON who died in Aberdeen 23RD June 1992 aged 83 years, and whose ashes were scattered here on her birthday 30TH June 1992. "Soul of my Soul, I shall meet thee again. With God be the Rest."

77. In loving memory of GEORGE GARDEN beloved husband of ELSIE CLARK who died at Lochs 6TH July 1929 aged 51 years. Also the said ELSIE CLARK who died at Lochs 19TH June 1946 aged 67 years. Also their daughter MARY (MOLLY) who died at Archiestown Hotel 29TH June 1975 aged 52 years. And also JOHN (JACK) who died at "Langbrae", Archiestown 24TH February 1997 aged 75 years.

78. Erected by JAMES M^cLENNAN in memory of his son ROBERT who died at Ardkelling, Blackhills Feb. 6TH 1903 aged 3 years 10^{mos}. Also JANE WILLIAMSON who died at Cotts, 11TH Jan. 1924 aged 59 years, wife of the said JAMES M^cLENNAN. And the said JAMES M^cLENNAN who died at Easter Cotts, 24TH February 1926 aged 66 years. Also their daughters JANE died 21ST Jan. 1992 aged 89 years. BETTY died 31ST March 1998 aged 94 years.

79. 1887. Erected by ALEXANDER M^cBETH in memory of his beloved wife MARGARET M^cINTOSH, who died 11th June 1882 aged 41 years, and of his children MARY, JOHN, & MARY who all died in infancy. Also of his aunt MARY SCOTT, who died 29th July 1887, aged 70 years.
(*Mason, W.T. Hendry, Abbey St., Elgin.*)

80. In loving memory of ALEXANDER WINCHESTER, who was accidentally killed at Viewfield, Urquhart, on the 18TH of Decr. 1895. Also his wife HELEN DAWSON who died at Tytler St., Forres, on the 20TH of May 1904. Also their daughter JANE WINCHESTER who died at Lochhill, Urquhart on

the 10TH of Octr. 1892. And their son JAMES, Master Mariner, who died at Forres 30TH Jan. 1938. Erected by their son JAMES.

80a. Treasured memories of NORMAN MATHIESON died 28TH July 2003 aged 81, loving dad of ALAN and dearly loved husband of MAY. Forever in our hearts.

81. 1899. In memory of ISABELLA SHANKS beloved wife of WILLIAM CAMERON who died at Longhill on 6TH May 1895, aged 80 years, and their son JAMES who died in infancy and the said WILLIAM CAMERON who died at Elgin on 3RD Augt. 1905, aged 84 years. "Asleep in Jesus".
(*Mason, Goodwillie, Elgin.*)

82. In loving memory of our dear mother CHRISTINA ROY, wife of W^M. CAMERON who did at Longhill 2ND Feb. 1914. Also the said W^M. CAMERON who died 20TH May 1930 aged 87 years. WILLIAM CAMERON 1865 – 1936. Erected by the family.

83. Erected to the memory of ALEXANDER LOGIE, who died at Urquhart, 25TH December 1888, aged 71 years. Also his spouse ANN YOUNG, who died 27TH January 1898, aged 85 years. Also their youngest daughter ELSPET who died at Bishopmill, 8TH April 1923, aged 70 years.
(*Mason, J. Young.*)

84. In loving memory of MARGARET INCH beloved wife of WILLIAM FORSYTH, Cranloch, who died 26TH Sept. 1885, aged 68 years. Also of the above WILLIAM FORSYTH, who died 14TH Decem. 1889 aged 72 years. And of their son JOHN FORSYTH, who died at Fowlis, Ross-shire, on 14TH October 1912, aged 70 years, and is interred at Dingwall. Also of their daughter MARGARET FORSYTH or ANDERSON who died at Evergreen 24TH January 1921 aged 82 years.
"I shall go to her but she shall not return to me."

84a. *Mason's Block.*
J. I.

85. Sacred to the memory of PETER BROWN, who occupied a croft at Moss of Meft, for nearly sixty years, was an elder in the church for more than the third of his life, and died 30TH Decr. 1859 aged 85. As also, to that of his wife, MARGARET FORSYTH, who after fulfilling with faithful attention her many duties in life died 22ND March 1849, aged 72, leaving three sons and three daughters to revere their memory.

86. Placed here by DONALD FRASER in memory of his beloved wife JANE BROWN who died at Urquhart 22. August 1858 aged 50 years.

87. Erected by JANE and ISABELLA BROWN in memory of their father JAMES BROWN sometime Farmer in Elginshill who died at Urquhart 6th Oc^t. 1840 Aged 91. Also their mother JANE REID who died 31st Decr. 1831

aged 58. Also their sister ELIZABETH who died 3ᵈ June 1831 aged 24. Also MAY who died 20th July 1812 aged 1 year.

87a.   *Mason's Block.*
       J. BRANDER.

88.   1881. Erected by JAMES & JOSEPH BRANDER in memory of their father DONALD BRANDER who died on the 20ᵀᴴ day of July 1869, aged 49 years. And their mother ISABELLA BROWN who died on the 5ᵀᴴ day of June 1868, aged 54 years. Also the said JAMES BRANDER who died at Leuchars, 23ᴿᴰ December 1891 aged 41 years. And his son ALEXANDER who died in infancy.
       (Mason, W.T. Hendry, Abbey St., Elgin.)

89.   Sacred to the memory of JAMES ROSS, Farmer, Whitehill, Lochinver, who departed this life on the 21ˢᵀ of June 1838, aged 51 years. And of his wife MARGARET BROWN, who died there 26ᵀᴴ May 1877, aged 82 years. Also their son JOHN, who died in the West Indies, 6ᵀᴴ May 1848, aged 31 years. And their son WILLIAM, who died also there, August 1852, aged 27 years. Take comfort, Christians, when your friends in Jesus fall asleep.
       Also ALEXANDER their son who died at Maryland, U.S.A., 21ˢᵀ July 1891, aged 71 years.
       (Mason, W.T. Hendry, Elgin.)

90.   Erected in loving memory of our sister MARGARET ROSS, who died suddenly at Innesmill, Urquhart, on the 4ᵀᴴ of January 1893, aged 70 years. Much loved, and deeply regretted. "At last we may each receive the welcome, well done, good and faithful servant, enter thou into the joy of thy Lord."
       (Mason, W.T. Hendry, Abbey St., Elgin.)

91.   In loving memory of my husband WILLIAM MACKAY died at Urquhart 17ᵀᴴ Dec. 1927 aged 78, also his wife MAXFIELD MACKAY died 30ᵀᴴ Aug. 1946 aged 95, their daughter MAXFIELD died 11ᵀᴴ April 1972 aged 87.
       (Mason, Robertson & Son, Hardgate, Aberdeen.)

92.   In memory of ALEXANDER P. MILNE died 17ᵀᴴ May 1938, aged 63. Also his wife ISABELLA MᶜKAY died 27ᵀᴴ March 1958, aged 80.

92a.   In loving memory of HARRY GOODBRAND 1928 – 2001, beloved husband of KAY SUTTON. Always remembered.
       (Mason, Robertson Memorials.)

93.   In loving memory of WILLIAM GOODBRAND who died 7ᵀᴴ April 1967 aged 74 years, and his beloved wife JESSIE MᴬᶜKAY who died 4ᵀᴴ July 1974 aged 81 years. Also their dear sons GORDON who died 5ᵀᴴ March 1940 aged 14 years. WILLIAM (Sgt. Air Gunner R.A.F.) killed 17ᵀᴴ Sept. 1944 aged 20 years, and GEORGE who died 13ᵀᴴ April 1949 aged 17 years. Till we meet.

94. *War Grave.* 1790117 Sergeant W. GOODBRAND Air Gunner Royal Air Force, 17TH September 1944 aged 20. "At the going down of the sun and in the morning we will remember him."

95. *Broken stone.*
Erected by JAMES FOULIS Moss of Meft in memory of his beloved daughter JANET FOULIS who died 12TH November? 1835/1855? aged 14 years. Also his beloved son WILLIAM FOULIS who died 5th March 1854, aged 36 years.

96. Sacred to the memory of ROBERT ANDERSON, Farmer, Viewfield who died 27TH May 1918, aged 73 years.

97. Sacred to the memory of WILLIAM ANDERSON, Farmer, Binns, who died 13TH March 1877, aged 74 years. Also of his son ALEXANDER, who died 1ST April 1840, aged 2 years. Also of ELIZABETH ASHER, wife of WILLIAM ANDERSON, who died 20TH July 1897, aged 90 years. And of their son JAMES ANDERSON, Farmer, Binns, who died 18TH Oct. 1908, aged 60 years. ANN BRANDER wife of JAMES ANDERSON who died 4TH Jany. 1925 aged 75 years. Their son W^{M} ALEXANDER died 14TH Sep. 1918, aged 33 years. Their daughter ANNIE who died 9TH Oct. 1961 aged 78 years. Their grandson JOHN died 11TH Aug. 1954 aged 48 years. Their grandson GEORGE died 12TH Sep. 1960 aged 54 years.

98. In memory of MARGARET ANDERSON the beloved wife of ROBERT SMITH who died 17TH April 1868, aged 28 years. "Jesus said I am the resurrection and the life "yet" Jesus wept".
(*Mason, T. Goodwillie.*)

99. Sacred to the memory of ROBERT ANDERSON, Ship Owner, Garmouth, who died on the 24TH day of February 1883 aged 79 years. "Blessed are they which do hunger and thirst after righteousness: for they shall be filled". Matthew 5 & 6.

100. Sacred to the memory of ALEXANDER ANDERSON, Ship Owner, Kingston, who died 4TH November 1876 aged 77 years. Also of his son ALEXANDER, Ship Master who died at Gibralter (*sic*) 24TH July 1867, aged 40 years. And of ANN SIMON, wife of the said ALEXANDER ANDERSON Senr. who died at Garmouth 2ND Feby. 1892, aged 94 years.

101. In loving memory of JOSEPH BROWN, aged 72, here interred Novr. 5TH 1866 & of HANNAH, his wife, interred at Brompton, London, 1862. "All pitying Jesu blest. Grant them thine eternal rest."

102. Erected by ALEX^{R} ELLIS in memory of his infant sons JAMES and ERNEST who died at Muiryhall, February 1893. Also of the said ALEX^{R} ELLIS, died at Woodside, Blackhills.

103. "The memory of the just is blessed , hear my prayer O Lord."

In loving memory of our dear father WILLIAM THIRD, who died Dec. 15TH 1895 aged 71 years. And our dear mother SUSAN HENDERSON, who died May 22ND 1896 aged 65 years.
(*Mason, W.T. Hendry.*)

104. In loving memory of GEORGE SCOTT NOBLE who died at Maverston, Urquhart, 5TH July 1936, aged 69 years. Also his wife MARGARET MELVIN who died at Maverston, Urquhart, 17TH April 1939, aged 69 years. Also their son JOHN beloved husband of ISABELL CAMPBELL who died at Oban 9TH April 1954, aged 55.
Flower holder. Worthy of Remembrance from GILBERT & GEORGE.
Flower holder. In memory of Father and Mother, from JIMMY.

105. Erected by JESSIE SCOTT, in memory of her beloved husband JOHN NOBLE, who died at Maverston 13TH June 1896, aged 67 years. Also the said JESSIE SCOTT, who died at Maverston 22ND March 1913 aged 93 years. And of their daughter ELIZA, who died at Beech View, Fochabers, on 10th February 1934, aged 81 years.
(*Mason, W.T. Hendry, Elgin.*)

106. Erected by ALEXANDER SCOTT, in memory of his father JAMES SCOTT, who died at Maverston 30TH March 1871, aged 79 years, and of his beloved mother ISABELLA DUNCAN, who died 6TH November 1876 aged 82 years. Also my sister ELIZABETH SCOTT. the said ALEX. SCOTT, died in 1924 aged 85 years.
(*Mason, T. Goodwillie.*)

107. 1871. Erected by WILLIAM SCOTT, (*M*)averstown, in memory of his daughter ISABELLA, who died 14TH January 1871, aged 25 years. Also of his beloved wife, HELLEN STEWART, who died 24TH June 1880, aged 66 years, and of their son, WILLIAM, who died 15TH January 1886, aged 32 years.

108. Erected by JOHN & JESSIE DOUGLAS, Castlehill, in loving memory of their children, ALEXANDER, died at Castlehill, 8TH Dec. 1878, aged 1 year. JESSIE died 26TH Oct. 1880, aged 9 years. ISABELLA died 1ST Nov. 1880, aged 8 years. JAMES died 20TH July 1897, aged 15 years. The said JOHN DOUGLAS died 10TH Feb.1919, aged 72 years. His wife JESSIE NOBLE died 12TH April 1937, aged 88 years. Their daughter MARY WATT DOUGLAS died 4TH July 1989, aged 98 years.
"The precious dust that lies beneath, shall at the call of Jesus rise."

109. Erected by JANE ANDERSON in memory of her husband JOHN MURDOCH, Farmer, Moss-side, Urquhart, who died 5TH April 1858, aged 57. Their son ALEXANDER who died 10TH July 1840, aged 6. Their daughter ELIZA who died 1ST April 1844 aged 6. And their son JAMES who died 1ST June 1867 aged 22. Also of the said JANE ANDERSON, who died at Moss-side, 29TH April 1879, aged 74. "Jesus wept."

110. In loving memory of MARY MURDOCH, who died at Hatton Cottage, Lhanbryde, 2ND March 1914, aged 62 years. Also JESSIE MURDOCH who died at Mary Park, Lhanbryde, 26th Nov. 1915, aged 71 years. Thy will be done.
(Mason, Hendry, Elgin.)

111. The memory of the just is blessed. In loving memory of WILLIAM MURDOCH, who died suddenly at Moss-side, Urquhart, 24TH May 1892, aged 57 years. Also ALEXANDER MURDOCH, who died at Orton, 23RD June 1911, aged 63 years.
(Mason, W.T. Hendry, Elgin.)

112. S.S.S. Erected in loving memory of JANE ANN MACKENZIE MACDONALD, loving wife and mother of JAMES & JAMES IAN MACBETH who died at Lynnwood Lodge, Lossiemouth 20TH March 1935 aged 53 years. Also the said JAMES MACBETH who died at Lynnwood Lodge, Lossiemouth 18TH Feb. 1955 aged 71 years, And their son JAMES IAN MACBETH 1921-1984, devoted husband to PETRICIA (*sic*) CLARK MAXWELL and loving father to his family

113. Erected by JAMES & ISABELLA MACBETH, Oakenhead, Drainie. In loving memory of their daughter ISABELLA, who died at Park Cottage, Lossiemouth 10TH May 1897 aged 16 years. Also their daughter ELIZA, who died at Oakenhead, 10TH Jany. 1913, aged 25 years. Also of the said JAMES MACBETH who died at Lynwood Lodge, Lossiemouth, 11TH Octr. 1923, aged 73 years. And of his wife ISABELLA NOBLE, who also died there, Sep^t. 5TH 1932 aged 76 years.
(Mason, W.T. Hendry.)

114a. S.S.S. Erected by HELEN ANN DONALD, in loving memory of her dear husband JOHN MACBETH, who died at Thornhill, Longmorn 9TH Aug. 1939 aged 60 years. Also the above HELEN ANN DONALD who died at Lynnwood Lodge, Lossiemouth, 17TH Sep^t. 1948 aged 55 years.

114b. S.S.S. Erected by ROBERT STUART MACBETH, Vancouver, B.C. in loving memory of his dear brother GEORGE who died in Vancouver B.C. 10TH Feb. 1948 as the result of wounds received in France 1914-1918 while serving with 1ST Canadian Expeditionary Force, aged 59 years. His ashes rest here.

114c. S.S.S. Erected by MINNIE BISSET in loving memory of her dear husband WILLIAM MACBETH who died at Cliff Terrace, Buckie, 27TH Jan. 1949 aged 64 years.

115. In memory of W_M. MARSHALL, Farmer, Unthank, died 23RD Aug. 1929 aged 75 years, also his wife JANE LAING died 19 July 1910 aged 55 years.

116. In loving memory of JAMES L. MARSHALL beloved husband of INA THOMSON died 11TH May 1959 aged 58 years. Also the said INA THOMSON died 19TH July 1987 aged 75 years.

117. Sacred to the memory of ALEXANDER FORSYTH third son of ANDREW FORSYTH, late Farmer in Broomhill of Innes, who died the 18/19th? day of January 1855, aged 35 years.

118. In loving remembrance of the late JAMES FORSYTH, Farmer, Broomhill, who died 17TH Oct. 1900 aged 83 years. Also his wife MARY HENDRY who died at Broomhill, 15TH Feb. 1902 aged 75 years.

119. Erected by J. & W. MACDONALD in loving memory of their father ALEXANDER MACDONALD, who died at Maverston, Urquhart 7TH January 1914 aged 84 years, and their mother JANE SIMPSON who died at Maverston 7TH September 1879 aged 51 years. Also their sister SOPHIA, who died at Maverston 9TH October 1914 aged 61 years, and their brother DAVID, who died at Elgin Hospital 15TH December 1881 aged 19 years. Also their sister ELIZABETH who died 13TH November 1947 aged 82 years. Also their youngest brother JAMES SIMPSON who died at Edinburgh 15TH August 1948 aged 85 years.

120. Erected by MARGARET CRAIG in memory of hir (*sic*) husband JAMES MAVER late Farmer in Blackhills who died March 1813 aged 49 years, and hir (*sic*) son ALEXANDER MAVER who died 26 July 1825 aged 11 years. Also the said MARGARET CRAIG who died on the 5th Octr. 1854 aged 82 years.

121. Erected by ISABELLA MAVOR in memory of her husband, WILLIAM MAVOR late farmer in Deanshaugh who died 10th June 1824 aged 55 years. WILLIAM MAVOR, their son, who died at Elgin, Illionios, (*sic*) United States, aged 29 years. Also the above ISABELLA MAVOR, who died at Woodlands, Bishopmill, 21st September 1862, aged 77 years.

122. In loving memory of MARGARET MARY GRANT daughter of C.M. GRANT, Viewfield, died 22 Sep. 1923 aged 9 years.

123. In loving memory of CHARLES MURDOCH GRANT, Farmer, Viewfield, born 4TH March 1877 died 24TH May 1936. And his daughter CHARLOTTE LESLEY, wife of L^T. G.F. DAVIDSON, R.E.4TH Oct^r.1941, aged 28 years. Also of his wife JANE PHILIP HARDIE died 19TH March 1973 aged 86 years. And his son CHARLES MURDOCH STRONACH died 3RD Oct. 1979 aged 68 years. And his wife MARY GRANT LINDSAY died 6TH March 1985 aged 74 years.

124. To the memory of WILLIAM KELLY who died at Urquhart June 25th 1846 in the 32nd year of his age. This stone is erected by ANN KELLY in token of the love and affection which she bore to her deeply regretted brother. Also of their father, ALEXANDER KELLY, who died at Urquhart, 13th Feby. 1862, aged 69 years. Also JANET YOUNG, beloved wife of ALEXANDER KELLY, who died 14TH March 1884 aged 88 years. Also JANET KELLY, who died 10TH April 1885 aged 60 years.

125. *Obelisk.*
     East face.
     In memory of CHRISTINA ANDERSON, beloved wife of JAMES BROWN, Ship-master, who died Jan. 26TH 1889 aged 38 years. Also of the said JAMES BROWN, who died at Burnside of Dipple 2ND June 1930 aged 83 years. "Forever with the Lord."
     North face.
     Also their son WILLIAM BROWN, died at Goodwood, 27TH Nov. 1945. And his wife MARY CATHERINE, died at Burnside of Dipple 5TH March 1948.

126. Sacred to the memory of MARY ANN SHAW, the beloved wife of GEORGE SMITH, Ship Master, Kingston, who died 19TH February 1869, aged 57 years. And GEORGE SMITH, Ship Master, late of Kingston, who died at Lossiemouth 10TH Nov[r]. 1885, aged 77 years.
     "She is not dead. But Sleepeth."
     (*Mason, J. Hendry, Elgin.*)

127. Erected by ALEXANDER ANDERSON, in memory of his father JAMES ANDERSON, Merchant in Kingston, who died 18TH January 1853, aged 66 years. Also of his wife, ELSPET REID, who died 25TH June 1861, aged 71 years, and also their son JAMES ANDERSON, who died at Aberdeen 8TH December 1883 aged 70 years. And also their daughter ISABELLA ANDERSON who died at Kingston 8TH October 1885, aged 58 years.
     (*Mason, J. Petrie, Aberdeen.*)

128. Erected by W[M] LOGIE, in loving memory of his wife MARJORY HUTCHEON who died at Mureyhall Oct. 16TH 1895 aged 73 years. Also of their son JOHN who died July 3RD 1857 aged 17 months. Also of the said WILLIAM LOGIE who died at Mureyhall Feb. 12TH 1900 aged 80 years. And their daughter ELSIE died at Goven (*sic*) Dec. 18TH 1901 aged 48 years. Interred in Craigton Cemetery.

129. Erected by ANDREW FORSYTH, Marine Engineer, in memory of his father WILLIAM FORSYTH Commission Agent, Lhanbryde who died 7TH April, 1899, aged 76 years. Also his wife ELSPETH M[c]GREGOR who died 20TH March 1907 aged 80 years.

130. In loving memory of JAMES DONALDSON Muiryhall, Lhanbryde died 16TH Feb. 1937 aged 73 years. And his beloved wife ANNIE MUNRO died 1ST May 1953 aged 88 years. Also their daughter JAMESINA died 17TH March 1999 aged 94 years.
     Flower holder. In loving memory.

131. In loving memory of ROBERT W. JAMIESON beloved husband of MARGARET DENOON who died at Seaview, Kingston 5TH Feb. 1946 aged 62 years. Also the said MARGARET DENOON who died 30TH Sep[t]. 1980 aged 82 years. And their daughter MARGARET JAMIESON who died 25TH June 1985 aged 59 years. JAMIESON.

132. Erected by ALEXANDER CATTACH, Urquhart, in memory of his son
WILLIAM who died 14ᵀᴴ May 1833 aged 1 year. His daughter ANN, who
died 10ᵀᴴ Novʳ. 1834 aged 5 years. Also his father JOHN CATTACH, who
died 10ᵀᴴ Febʸ. 1842 aged 84 years. And his mother ELSPET PAUL who
died 14ᵀᴴ May 1843 aged 82 years, also his daughter MARGARET, who died
Oct. 2, 1850, aged 16, and also his wife ANN SMART, who died Augᵗ. 13,
1851, aged 58.

133. Erected by GEORGE ANDERSON, in loving memory of his wife
MARGARET ROY who died 1ꜱᴛ March 1910 aged 48 years. Also their
daughter JOANNA who died in infancy. Also of the said GEORGE
ANDERSON who died at The Anchorage, Lossiemouth 19ᴛʜ May 1939 aged
79 years.

134. 1899. Erected by GEORGE MᶜKIDD in loving memory of his wife JESSIE
MUNRO or MᶜKIDD, who died at Moss of Meft 11ᵀᴴ March 1898, aged 59
years, and of their children ISABELLA ELLEN, who died 16ᵀᴴ Decʳ. 1883,
aged 12 years and MAGGIE, who died 5ᵀᴴ May 1886, aged 13 years. Also of
the said GEORGE MᶜKIDD, who died 20ᵀᴴ Febʸ. 1906, aged 69 years.
"Asleep in Jesus".
(*Mason, W.H. Goodwillie, Elgin.*)

135. Sacred to the memory of our dear son ROBERT GEORGE ANDERSON,
who died at Lhanbryde, 3ᴿᴰ April 1914, aged 6 years. "Jesus called a little
child unto him."
(*Mason, W.T. Hendry.*)

136. Erected by ANN MᶜKIDD, House Keeper, at Pitgaveny, in memory of
JOSEPH MᶜKIDD her brother who died at Urquhart on the 7ᵗʰ of May 1921
aged 20 years.

137. In loving memory of WILLIAM CALDWELL, Cranloch, died 6ᵀᴴ Feb. 1937
aged 22 years.

138. In memory of HENDRY SCOTT, Cranloch, who died 15ᵀᴴ August 1870,
aged 63 years, also of his wife, MARGARET MILNE, who died 23ᴰ January
1867, aged 58 years. Erected by their family And of their son JAMES
SCOTT who died 5ᵀᴴ Febʸ. 1902, aged 65 years. Also JOHN SCOTT who
died at Cranloch, 12ᵀᴴ May 1915 aged 76 years. And their son GEORGE
SCOTT who died at Cranloch, 4ᵀᴴ Sepᵗ. 1920 aged 74 years. ELSPET
MᶜKISSACK died 27ᵀᴴ Dec. 1930 aged 87 years. And of his mother
MARGARET DINGWALL, who died 24ᵀᴴ January 1858, aged 73 years.
(*Mason, T. Goodwillie.*)

139. Erected by JOHN ROBB, in Lhanbryde, in memory of his sons. JAMES,
who died in August 1845, aged 8 months. GEORGE, who died in March
1848, aged 14 months. Also of his son ALEXANDER, who died on 7ᵀᴴ
March 1867, aged 24 years. Also of his son FREDERICK, who died 9ᵀᴴ
December 1881, aged 22 years. His wife ELSPIT ADAM who died Feb.

1902. "Make haste, impr.... and don't delay: death in my prime, took me away". "Much loved, much mourned." (*Mason, Hendry, Elgin.*)

139a. *Mason's Block.*
Blank.

140. In loving memory of our father JOHN ROBB, who died at Wester Coxton 11TH Nov. 1916 aged 74 years. Also his family JOHN who died July 1869 aged 2 years. ELIZABETH, who died Nov. 1883 aged 12 years. ALEXANDER who died Nov. 1883 aged 2 years. CHARLES who died July 1890 aged 2 years. ELSIE who died Dec. 1890 aged 21 years. KATE who died at Rosario, S.A. 20TH Jan. 1918 aged 38 years, the wife of R. WHITE, Buenos Aires. ELIZABETH CRAIGMYLE, wife of JOHN ROBB died at Woodside, Lhanbryde, 10TH Dec. 1930 aged 84.

141. 1856. Erected by WILLIAM MUNRO, Landsend of Urquhart, in memory of his daughter, ISABEL MUNRO, who died 7th July 1856, aged 29 years. Also his spouse JANE SUTHERLAND, who died 11th April 1863, aged 79. The said WILLIAM MUNRO died 2nd Decr. 1870, aged 83.

142. Erected in memory of ARCHIBALD MELVIN, Postman from Elgin to Urquhart for 22 years, died 13th June 1886, aged 57 years. Also his daughter ANNE, who died at Birchfield Urquhart, 19TH Nov. 1910, aged 58 years. Also his wife HELEN ANDERSON, who died at Birchfield, Urquhart, 21ST June 1914, aged 84 years. "Rest in peace thou beloved." Also their son JAMES ADAM MELVIN died at Redbog 14TH July 1919 aged 56 years. And EDWARD ARCHIBALD MELVIN died at Cranloch 24TH Dec. 1938 aged 63 years. AGNES youngest daughter died at Elgin 2ND May 1943 aged 70 years. To live in hearts we leave behind, is not to die.
(*Mason, T. Goodwillie.*)

143. Erected to the memory of ISABELLA ANDERSON spouse to ALEXANDER ANDERSON, Farmer in Branstown, who died 31st March 1838 aged 69 years. This stone is placed here by her sons.

144. Erected to the memory of ALEXANDER ANDERSON late Farmer in Branstown who died 10th May 1827 aged 82 years. This stone is placed here by his sons.

145. Erected by ROBERT ASHER, Carpenter, in memory of his son GEORGE ASHER, Engineer, who died 18th March 1868 aged 26.

145a. *Mason's Block.*
R. ASHER.

146. Erected by JANNET CRAMOND to the memory of her beloved husband ALEXANDER CAMERON, Ship Carpenter, Garmouth, who died 19th April 1840 aged 47 years. Also their daughter JESSIE who died in infancy. Also their sons JOHN CAMERON, Carpenter, who died the 10th Sep^t. 1852 aged 21 years. And JAMES CAMERON, Seaman who died 23^d Feby. 1858 aged

24 years. Also the above JANNET CRAMOND who died the 4th April 1883 aged 83 years.

147. Erected by PHILIP GRIGHTON (*sic*), (*CRIGHTON*) Shipmaster, in memory of his beloved wife JESSIE CAMERON, who died 5TH August 1867, aged 28 years. Also of the said PHILIP CRIGHTON, Shipmaster, who died 4TH Feby. 1909, aged 69 years. In memory also of JANET ANN CRIGHTON, their daughter who died 7TH April 1938, aged 71 years, and who was interred in Elgin Cemetery.
(*Mason, J. Hendry, Elgin.*)

148. *Flat Stone.*
Erected in memory of WALTER LOGIE, Ship Builder, at Garmouth who died 7th April 1835 aged 66 years, and also his spouse ANN GRANT who died 7th April 1834/1854?, aged 80 years.

149. Erected by JAMES SIMPSON, in memory of his beloved wife MARY HENDRY who died at Urquhart 25TH July 1905 aged 32 years. Also his sons, JAMES PHIMISTER who died 23RD Jany. 1909 aged 3 months. JAMES GERRIE who died 24TH Feby. 1910 aged 5 months. Also his second wife JEANNIE PHIMISTER who died 4TH Decr. 1910, aged 27 years. Also of the said JAMES SIMPSON who died 18TH Decr. 1939 aged 65 years. Sadly missed. And CATHERINE M^cGREGOR wife of the above JAMES SIMPSON, who died 7TH Dec. 1961 aged 85 years.

150. Erected in memory of WILLIAM MUNRO who died at Urquhart the 20th May 1844 aged 101 years, also his spouse ELSPET GEDDES who died April 1791 aged 48 years. This stone is placed here by there (*sic*) daughter MARY MUNRO. Also the said MARY MUNRO, who deid (*sic*) April 16th 1858, aged 89 years.

151. 1911. Erected by GEORGE EDWARDS, and family in memory of his beloved wife JANE CROMBIE, who died at Templand, Lhanbryde, 7TH March 1911, aged 80 years. And their son JAMES, who died as the result of an accident, at G.N.S.R. Station, Craigellachie, 26TH Octr. 1906, aged 39 years. Also the above GEORGE EDWARDS, who died at Templand, Lhanbryde, 12TH Feby. 1919, aged 84 years.
(*Mason, W.T. Hendry, Elgin.*)

152. In loving memory of my dear husband DAVID EDWARDS who died at Lhanbryde 27TH March 1947 aged 73 years. Also his beloved wife JANE MILNE who died 19TH Oct. 1975 aged 82 years.
Flower holder. In loving memory.

153. Erected by JANE & ANN CROMBIE, in loving memory of their mother JANE KELLY, who died 6TH Sept. 1875 aged 78 years. Also their father DAVID CROMBIE, who died 1ST July 1885 aged 90 years.
"Gone but not forgotten."

154. In loving memory of our father DAVID CROMBIE who died at Clatternbriggs 3RD Jan. 1925. Also our mother JESSIE FRASER who died 27TH Dec. 1924. And our sister ANN who died in infancy. And our brother WILLIAM who died 1ST Feb. 1963 aged 80 years. And his wife JESSIE ANN HAY who died 19TH March 1987 aged 93 years.
Flower holder. In loving memory.

155. *Stone marked on 1978 plan but no inscription recorded in 1978 survey, no stone now visible.*

156. Erected by ALEXANDER CROMBIE, in loving memory of his wife ELSPET MILNE, who died at Lhanbryde, on 25TH May 1913, aged 76 years. Also the said ALEXANDER CROMBIE, who died at Leuchars, 25TH May 1915, aged 80 years.
(Mason, W.T. Hendry, Elgin.)

157. Erected by JOHN CROMBIE, in loving memory of his father ROBERT CROMBIE, who died at Leuchars, Aug'. 1843. Also his mother MARJORY ANDERSON, who died at Arabella, Ross-shire, 4TH Aug'. 1877. Also the said JOHN CROMBIE, who died at Leuchars 19TH Jan'. 1919, aged 80 years. And his wife ELIZABETH CRAMOND, who died at Leuchars 28TH Jan'. 1933 aged 93 years. Also their son JOHN who died at Aberdeen 17TH Jan. 1937 aged 71 years. And their daughter MARGARET WALKER who died at Leuchars 6TH Aug. 1941 aged 74 years.
(Mason, W.T. Hendry, Elgin.)

158. In memoriam. MARGARET ANDERSON, beloved wife of WILLIAM COOK, Binns, Urquhart, died December 22ND 1878, aged 78 years. Also of the above WILLIAM COOK, who died 12TH January 1882, aged 86 years. Also their daughter ANN, who died at Lhanbryde, 6TH June 1919 aged 90 years.

159. Erected by ANN COOK in memory of her father JOHN COOK who died at Unthank 24th August 1824 aged 62 years. Her brother JAMES who died 29th November 1826 aged 22 years. Her mother ANN INNES who died 8th November 1843 aged 80 years. And of her sister ELSPETH who died at Cotts of Innes 27th July 1864 aged 72 years. Also of the above ANN COOK who died at the Village of Duffus 13th July 1875, in the 82nd year of her age.

160. Erected in loving memory of their parents GEORGE COOK, Farmer, who died at Unthank 9TH January 1879 aged 78 years. Also their mother ANN PANTON who died at Ellon, Aberdeenshire 4TH September 1882 aged 74 years. Also their brothers, JAMES who died at Melbourne, Australia, 24TH July 1876 aged 38 years. ROBERT who died at Georgetown, Demerara, 2ND April 1883 aged 32 years. GEORGE who died at Buckie 21ST August 1886 aged 44 years. JOHN who died at Hills, Urquhart, 10TH May 1890 aged 54 years. JANE who died in infancy. JESSIE COOK died at Lhanbryde 15TH October 1915 aged 71 years.

161.   Erected by ANN FINDLAY in memory of her beloved mother JANE COOK who died at Cranloch Novr. 16th 1863 aged 63.

162.   In memory of WILLIAM COOK, Farmer, Milton, died 16TH May 1914, aged 83. Also his wife AMELIA EMILY McGILLIVRAY died 19TH April 1912, aged 75. Also their family Isabella, died 12TH July 1908, aged 46. WILLIAM, died 13TH August 1888, aged 22. JOHN, died 6TH Decr. 1912, aged 43. ALEXANDER, died 1ST May 1877, aged 6. ROBERT ANDERSON, died 4TH May 1877, aged 4. MARGARET ANDERSON died 13TH Dec. 1925, aged 61. AMELIA B.M. COOK youngest daughter died 2ND May 1943, aged 67. And JAMES COOK, Farmer, died 24TH May 1947, aged 79.

163.   Erected by ROBERT CAMERON in memory of his beloved wife JANE REID who died at Urquhart, 9TH Jany. 1903, aged 29 years. Also their daughter MARGARET JANE who died 4TH Feby. 1903 aged 10 months. And of the said ROBERT C. CAMERON, who died 3RD May 1925, aged 52 years.

163a.   *Mason's Block.*
R. C.

164.   *Table stone, very worn.*
Here are interred the remains of MARGARET MILNE who died at Urquhart on the 10 day of May 18?? In the 56th year of her age. This stone is erected to her memory by her affectionate spouse WILLIAM ROY who died 12th Agust (*sic*) 18(*??*) aged 72 years. And their son ROBERT who died 9th Sep^t. 1889(*?*) aged 29 years. Also his son GEORGE ROY who died at Urquhart the 7th of August 1855 aged 73. Also of MARGARET REID his wife who died on 6th Nov^r.1867 aged 75.

165.   Erected by JANE PYPER, in memory of her beloved husband WILLIAM ROY, Mason, who died on 26TH June 1829. Also of their daughter who died in infancy. And of their son WILLIAM, who died at Urquhart on 2ND May 1843, aged 16 years. Also of the said JANE PYPER or ROY, who died in Elgin on 25TH December 1882, aged 81 years.

166.   *Obelisk.*
East face.
ALEXANDER.   In loving memory of my father THOMAS GORDON ALEXANDER who died in Aberdeen 1904 and interred here. And of my mother ANNIE M^{c}HARDY who died 1883, interred in Rafford Churchyard. My sister CHRISTINA M^{c}GREGOR died in 1938, interred Forest Home Cemetery, Illinois, U.S.A. And of her daughter ANNE ELIZABETH GELLATLY died 1944, interred Lawndale Cemetery, Illinois, U.S.A. Also my beloved brother JOHN M^{c}HARDY, who died at Rosebrae, Sep. 25. 1952. Also of my sister SUSANNA M^{c}HARDY, who died in Glasgow Jan. 16. 1954 and is interred here. "Until the day dawn, and the shadows flee away."
South face.
ALEXANDER.   In loving memory of our grand-parents ROBERT ALEXANDER who died in Urquhart 1890, and ELIZABETH SMITH, who died in 1897. Also of my father ROBERT ALEXANDER died at Little

Bogton 1941, and my mother BATHIA DOUGLAS, died at Rosebrae, 1946. Also my brother JOHN M^CHARDY, died in Gray's Hospital, Elgin. 1927. And my sister BATHIA DOUGLAS died at Little Bogton, 1934. Also of PATRICK DOUGLAS ALEXANDER, Rosebrae, died in Gray's Hospital, Elgin, May 16, 1955.
North face.
ALEXANDER. Sacred to the memory of MARGARET ROSE, 1st wife of ROBERT ALEXANDER who died in 1848. And of her son HUGH, who died in 1910. Both interred here.

167. Erected by THOMAS M^cKINZIE, Longhill, in rememberance (sic) of his daughter MARY, who died on the 30th day of April 1853, aged 1 year. Also the said THOMAS M^cKINZIE, who died at Rutherhill, Moss of Meft, 7th April 1896, aged 78 years.

167a. *Mason's Block.*
J. C.

168. In memory of JOHN CHALMERS who died 18TH April 1901. Also his wife ELISABETH PHIN who died 23RD June 1941 aged 34 years. And their family ANNIE & JAMES. Also his son JOHN who died 24TH June 1909, and his daughter MARY who died 11TH Jan. 1922 aged 75 years.

169. Erected by MARGARET NEISH, in memory of her husband JOHN NEISH, who died at Woodpark on the 21ST day of March 1877, aged 65 years.
(Mason, W.T. Hendry, Elgin.)

170. In loving memory of my sister ELIZABETH TAYLOR, born at Clockeasy, Urquhart, died at Urquhart Villa, Lossiemouth, 7TH May 1934 aged 76. Erected by ELSIE TAYLOR Urquhart Villa, Lossiemouth, born 9TH March 1865, died 1ST November 1951, also interred here.

171. *Flat Stone.*
Sacred to the memory of ANN BARRON, who died 7th Augt. 1834 aged 8 years. Also her father JOHN BARRON who died at Bishopmill 23rd May 1853 aged 60 years. Also his son JAMES BARRON who died the 19th April 1861 aged 25 years. Also SARAH DONALDSON, their mother who died at Bishopmill 28th January 1891, aged 86 years. Also MARGARET BARRON their daughter who died at Bishopmill 25th May 1903 aged 78 years.
Placed here by JOHN BARRON, Mason.

172. Erected by SARAH FRASER in memory of her sister MARGARET BARRON, wife of JAMES LOGIE, who died at Bishopmill, 25TH May 1903, aged 78 years. Also of the said JAMES LOGIE, who died 20TH Novr. 1904 aged 82 years.
(Mason, W.T. Hendry, Elgin.)

173. 1849. Erected to the memory of JAMES DONALDSON, late Farmer in Urquhart, who died 18th February 1845, aged 79 years. Also his spouse MARGARET YOUNG who died 30th August 1850, aged 82 years.

174. To the memory of JAMES DONALDSON, Farmer, Urquhart, who died 8TH May 1872 aged 77 years. Also his son JOHN DONALDSON, Farmer, Urquhart, who died 23RD Nov. 1919 aged 23 years. Also his wife ELSPETH CHALMERS who died 4TH June 1912 aged 73 years. Also their sons THOMAS who died 31ST Jan. 1892 aged 9 years. PETER who died at Glasgow 13TH Oct. 1918 aged 41 years. JOHN who died at Edinburgh 2ND Aug. 1934 aged 60 years. Also their daughter-in-law MARY SIMPSON beloved wife of WILLIAM DONALDSON who died in Greenock Hospital, 24TH Jan. 1951 aged 65 years. Cremated at Paisley. Also the above WILLIAM DONALDSON who died at Newton Mearns 29TH May 1958 aged 82 years.

175. Here lies the body of THOMAS BRANDER son of W^{M} BRANDER late in Finfan, who died 30 Oct. 1797 aged 23 years. Also HELLEN BRANDER who died 19 I(*J*)an. 1795 aged 25 years. And IANNET BRANDER who died 27 I(*J*)an. 1791 aged 16 years.

176. This stone is erected by BARBARA M^{c}KENZIE to the memory of her husband GEORGE BRANDER who departed this life the 17th Septr. 1835 aged (*33?*) years.

177. Erected by JAMES BRANDER, Shipmaster, Kingston. In memory of his sisters, JANET BRANDER, who died 4th July 1833, aged 7 months. And JESSY BRANDER, who died 25th Septr. 1858, aged 20 years. Also of his father THOMAS BRANDER, Shipmaster, who died at Shields, on the 12th October 1850, aged 50 years. And of his mother, HELLEN SIMPSON, who died at Kingston, on the 17 or 18th (*sic*) January 1870, aged 70 years. ISABELLA BRANDER, died at Stotfield, Lossiemouth, 5th Oct. 1906. Her husband WILLIAM DENOON, lost at sea, 25th Sepr. 1869.
(*Mason, W.M. Forsyth, Sculp., Elgin.*)

178. Sacred to the memory of WILLIAM CHALMERS, Muriehall, who died 27th Sep^{t}. 1871, aged 62 years, also his wife, MARY M^{c}DONALD, who died 30th July 1861, aged 45 years, and their daughters, JANET, who died in infancy, and ISABELLA, who died 17th May 1860, aged 16 years. Also their son JAMES, who died at Carnoustie, in the 24th year of his age. Also MARGARET FLETCHER, wife of his son WILLIAM, who died at Muriehall, 27th Novr. 1915 aged 73 years. Also the said WILLIAM CHALMERS died at Muriehall, 12th March 1923 in his 78th year.

179. In loving memory of our dear father and mother. Our father, JAMES ARCHIBALD, who died at Moss of Barmuckity 26th Aug. 1883, aged 38 years. Also our dear mother ISABELLA BRANDER who died at Maverston, Urquhart 27th Jan. 1915, aged 67 years. Also their daughter, ISABELLA who died at Maverston Aug. 31st 1927, aged 54 years. Also their sons, WILLIAM who died at Dr. Gray's Hospital 22nd Feb. 1950, aged 73 years. JAMES who died at Maverston 1st Sep^{t}. 1953, aged 79 years, beloved husband of MARY WINTON.

180. Erected by WILLIAM FRASER, in memory of his father WILLIAM FRASER, who died at Urquhart 28th July 1859 aged 59 years. Also his mother MARGARET PHEMISTER, who died at Urquhart, 15th April 1880 aged 73 years, and his brother ALEXANDER who died at Edinburgh, 19th Nov[r]. 1869 aged 27 years. And their grand-children, JANE FINDLAY, aged 6 years, and ELIZABETH aged 2 years, who both died at Urquhart May 1869.
(Mason, W.T.Hendry, Abbey St., Elgin.)

181. Sacred to the memory of BARBARA ABBERCROMBIE, *(sic)* the beloved wife of ROBERT SMITH, Gardener, Innes, who departed this life 23[d] August 1863 aged 42. Also their son ANDREW who died 26th March 1863 aged 12. ROBERT SMITH, husband of the above, died at Innes House 1st August 1866. Also their son JAMES SMITH died at Innes House 20th September 1876 aged 32 years. Also their son ALEXANDER A. SMITH who died at Innes House 12th Nov. 1902 aged 56 years.

182. Erected by GEORGE PATTERSON, Clothier, Urquhart, in loving memory of his children, GEORGINA died 6TH March 1884, aged 13 days. ROBERT died 6TH July 1889, aged 1 year & 10 months. JAMES CANT died 21ST Nov[r]. 1891 aged 1 year & 6 months. THOMAS died in infancy 13TH February 1893. MARY ANN S. died 23RD November 1898, aged 21 years. ELSIE, died 6TH February 1910 aged 14 years. ALEXANDER, died at Krugerdorp, S.A. 21ST May 1928 aged 52 years. Also his wife ELIZABETH PATERSON *(sic)* died 7TH July 1929 aged 78 years. Also the above GEORGE PATTERSON died at Aberdeen, 17TH August 1931, aged 79 years.
(Mason, Goodwillie, Elgin.)

183. 1878. SIC TRANSIT GLORIA MUNDI. Erected in memory of FRANCIS HENDRY, who died at Newfield, on the 31st May 1877, aged 72 years. And of his wife, ISABELLA RUSSELL, who died 13th December 1885 aged 85 years.
(SIC TRANSIT GLORIA MUNDI, translation; so passes away earthly glory.)

183a. "He sleeps where none can mourn & weep." Dedicated to the dear memory of JOHN DEAN who fell asleep on 4TH July 1914 aged 27 years. He sleeps at Ellensdale, Rhodesia, S.A.

184. In loving memory of ALEXANDER TAYLOR, Farmer, Lachlanwells, Alves, who died 26TH Jan[y]. 1901 aged 69 years. Also of his son ROBERT ANDERSON TAYLOR, M.A. Medical student, who died 18TH Feb[y]. 1904 aged 22 years. And also his wife, JANET ANDERSON who died 22ND May 1909 aged 73 years.

185. Erected by WILLIAM M[c]KENZIE, Merchant, Urquhart, in memory of his daughter MARGARET, who died in infancy. Also his beloved wife, ISABELLA SINCLAIR, who died at Bogmoor, 2ND April 1916 aged 69 years, also his grand-daughter, ANNIE SINCLAIR DOUGLAS, died 4TH April 1916 aged 11 days, interred together. Also the said, WILLIAM M[c]KENZIE, who died at Bogmoor, 1ST May 1916 aged 76 years. Also his son

WILLIAM who died at Foresterhill 14TH Feb. 1969, aged 84 years, and his wife ELSIE STEPHEN who died 26TH March 1972 in her 90th year. And MARY ELDER CRAIK died 3RD Aug. 1979 aged 68, dear wife of their son WILLIAM died 23RD April 1985 aged 77, interred in Lair 400 new cemetery.
(Mason, T.Goodwillie),
(Mason, W.T. Hendry, Elgin.)
Two mason's names on stone, one on either face.

186. Erected by ALEXANDER BRANDER, Farmer, Lochs, in memory of his beloved wife ISABELLA FORSYTH, who died on the 2ND of April 1883, aged 72 years. And his daughter JESSIE, who died on the 21ST of May 1863 aged 17 years. And the said ALEXANDER BRANDER, who died on the 11TH of May 1899 aged 90 years. And his son JAMES, M.B.C.M., Aberdeen University, who died at Aberdeen, 9TH February 1913, aged 68 years. Also his daughter MARGARET ELIZABETH born 1857, died 1929.
(Mason, A. Robertson, King St., Abdn.)

187. *East Face.*
To the memory of WILLIAM BRANDER Farmer, Ferniefield, born 1845, died 1918, also his widow* ISABELLA BRANDER, born 1847, died 1930. Their son ALEXANDER, who died in infancy. Their daughter MARGARET ELIZABETH, born 1870, died 1950. Their son WILLIAM BRANDER, Farmer, Ferniefield, born 1873, died 1951. Their daughter ISABELLA BRANDER, born 1876, died 1970.
**The word 'wife' has been overwritten 'widow'*
South Face.
To the memory of WILLIAM BRANDER, Farmer, Ferniefield, born 7TH May 1804, died 15TH April 1856, and of his wife ANN REID, born 11TH June 1811, died 10TH Sep^t. 1903, also to the memory of their children,
JAMES, born 1835, died 1848.
MARY ANN, born 1851, died 1853.
ROBINA, born 1847, died 1869.
ELEANOR JANE, born 1853, died 1882.
ISABELLA, born 1833, died 1887.
JEMIMA, born 1849, died 1905.
JESSIE, born 1843, died 1906.
ANNIE, born 1835, died 1918.
WILLIAM, born 1845, died 1918.
ELIZABETH, born 1842, died 1922.
MARGARET, born 1837, died 1935.
ALEX^R JAMES, born 1855, died 1945.
North Face.
To the memory of WILLIAM BRANDER, Farmer, Ferniefield, born 1873, died 1951. And his wife MARGARET I.R. MILNE, born 28TH Sept. 1888, died 2ND Nov. 1975.

188. In memory of CATHERINE MACKENZIE, wife of W. ROYAN died 25TH Aug. 1920 aged 41.

189.   Here lies the body of WILLIAM BRANDER, son of W^M BRANDER, late in Finfan, who died 26 I(J)uly 1795 aged 25 years and JEAN BRANDER who died 24 I(J)une 1794 aged 17 years.

190.   1896. Sacred to the memory of JOHN CHRISTIE, who died at Blackhills, in 1848 aged 44. Also his spouse, HELLEN PYPER, who died at Lhanbryde 1892 aged 89 years. Much regretted by all who knew her.

191.   Erected by WILLIAM and JOHN CALDER in memory of their parents MARGARET M^cCAGIE who died at Moss of Barmuckity 2^d July 1828 aged 28 years. And GEORGE CALDER who died 28th April 1849 aged 52 years.

192.   DENOON. Erected by JAMES DENOON, Lossiemouth, in loving memory of his mother CHRISTINA URQUHART, who died at Meft on the 13th Oct. 1852, aged 39 years. And of his father JOHN DENOON, who died at Urquhart, on the 26th Feb. 1896, aged 80 years. Also of his brothers, WILLIAM, lost overboard in the North Sea off the Naze of Norway on the 21st Sept. 1868, aged 27 years. GEORGE, buried at sea off the Canary Islands on the 30th Sept. 1877, aged 28 years. JOHN M^cPHERSON, Master of the Ship Garmouth, supposed run down with all hands in the Bay of Biscay, Nov. 1879, aged 43 years. ALEXANDER and GEORGE who died in infancy. "And the sea gave up the dead which were in it." Rev. 20.13.

193.   Erected by JOHN DENOON, in memory of his mother ELSIE M^cWILLIAM, who died at Urquhart 14th Dec. 1899, aged 73.

193a. *Mason's Block.*
       A. ALLAN.

194.   1853.   Erected in memory of ALEXANDER ALLAN, sometime Miller at Innesmill who died 13th Decr. 1849, aged 89 years, and his spouse MARGARET ROBERTSON who died 18th Jany. 1818, aged 52 years. Also their daughter MARY who died 10th Jany. 1806 aged 1 year. ANN who died 13th June 1817, aged 23 years. Also their son JOHN who died at Dundee 13th July 1824, aged 27 years. This stone is placed here by ALEXANDER ALLAN, their son, and JOHN ROSS their son in law.

195.   Erected by ALEXANDER ALLAN in memory of his children, GEORGE who died 20th Decr. 1833 aged 2 years, also MARY who died 6th Jany. 1850, aged 25 years. And of the said ALEXANDER ALLAN who died at Lochs on the 11TH Feby. 1864, aged 74 years. And JANE FORSYTH, his wife, who died 27TH June 1883, aged 88 years. ROBERT, died 6th March 1876, aged 48 years.

196.   Erected by JOHN ARCHIBALD to the memory of his children ANN who died 10th July 1828 aged 2 years. And ROBERT who died 1st Sepr. 1846 aged 9 years. And GEORGE who died 1st Feby. 1850 aged 21 years. Also of JOHN ARCHIBALD their father, who died at Lochs, Sept. 25th 1873, aged 84 years. And MARGARET ALLAN, his wife, who died Febr. 5th 1873, aged 82 years. Also their Grandchild JESSIE SHAND, beloved wife of A.

M^cKENZIE, who died at Lochs 4th April 1900 aged 35 years. "Until the day dawn."

196a. *Mason's Block.*
ALEX^R ARCHIBALD.

197. 1903. In loving memory of our dear father ARTHUR ARCHIBALD, Mason, who died at Lochs, on the 17TH Sep^t. 1902, aged 50 years. Also our dear brother JAMES, who died, Aug. 21ST 1902 aged 16 years. Also MARY ANN daughter of the said ARTHUR ARCHIBALD and beloved wife of W^M CHEYNE who died at Lochs, Urquhart 25TH April 1930 aged 49 years. Also our dear mother MARY ANN M^cLEAN who died 1ST Aug. 1938 aged 81 years. And our dear sister JESSIE MILNE who died 15TH June 1938. Erected by ARTHUR ARCHIBALD.

198. Sacred to the memory of ROBERT BAIN Esqr, Writer in Elgin, who died there on 21st July 1846, aged 64. This stone has been erected here by a few of his personal friends, as a token of their sincere regard.

199. In loving memory of JAMES WINCHESTER beloved child of JOHN & ISABELLA DEAN, born 18TH Augt. 1889 died 16TH May 1892 "How lovely is thy dwelling place."

200. In loving memory of JAMES WINCHESTER, Mason, the village-of-Urquhart, born at Covesea, 12TH April 1817, died at Urquhart, 12TH Jany. 1883 aged 65. His wife HELEN BAIN, who died 30TH Novr. 1885, aged 72. Also their son JOHN, aged 3. Also their daughter JANE, who died in London, aged 40. And their son JAMES, who died at Durban, Africa, 15TH Feby. 1896, aged 42. And their daughters HELEN and CHRISTINA who both died in London. And ISABELLA who died 27TH Aug. 1930, aged 78. Also her husband JOHN DEAN who died 20TH Oct. 1929, aged 84. And ISABELLA JANE, youngest daughter of JOHN and ISABELLA DEAN who died 17TH Feb. 1974, aged 94. "They have met to part, never till the resurrection dawn."

201. Erected by the family in loving memory of WILLIAM TAYLOR, Clockeasy died 5TH Aug. 1888, aged 77 years. Also his wife, ELSPET M^cCONNACHIE died 24TH Aug. 1901, aged 75 years.

202. Erected by ALEXANDER TAYLOR, Farmer, Tippertait in memory of his daughter JANE, who died 18TH October, 1845, aged 16 years. And of his daughter MARGARET, who died 1ST October, 1838, aged 2 years. Also of his son JAMES late Free Church Teacher, Cromarty, who died 30TH December, 1873 aged 32 years. Also of his beloved wife, JANE SIMON, who died 17TH November 1882, aged 78 years. And also of the said ALEXANDER TAYLOR, who died 30TH January 1888, aged 85 years.

203. Erected by COSMO REID, Farmer, Gladhill, to the memory of his brother James, who died 4th March 1841, aged 10 months. Also of his father, COSMO REID, late Farmer in Gladhill, who died there 10th June 1850, aged 56 years. And of his sister, ISOBELLA, who died 8th June 1850, aged 21

years. ELISABETH, who died 17th Jan[ry]. 1852, aged 15 years. MARGARET, who died 20th Jan[ry]. 1852 aged 17 years. GEORGE REID, who died at Gealong (*sic*), Australia, 18th May 1861, aged 28 years. Also of COSMO REID, Farmer, Gladhill, who died 19th January 1869, aged 37 Years. Also of MARGARET SMITH, his mother, the beloved wife of COSMO REID, who died at Loanhead, 23rd October 1880 aged 78 years.

204. Erected by JOHN REID, Gladhill, in loving memory of his daughter ISABELLA, wife of C.C. FRASER who died at Ilford 5TH Nov. 1914, aged 38 years. And the said JOHN REID who died at Laburnum, Garmouth 17TH Dec. 1931 aged 86 years. And his wife MARGARET BROWN who died at Laburnum 13TH June 1932 aged 88 years. REID.
(*Mason, Wilson, Elgin.*)

205. Sacred to the memory of my dear husband Major WILLIAM G. ASHCROFT 7TH Seaforth Hrs. who was killed in Normandy 28TH June 1944 aged 39 years. He laid on duty's altar the greatest gift of all his life.

205a. *Mason's Block.*
J. S.

206. In memory of the Rev[d] WILLIAM GORDON, who was inducted minister of Urquhart on the 12TH January 1769, and died on the 18th July 1810, in the 67TH year of his age, of MARGARET ANDERSON his wife (daughter of the Rev[d] JOSEPH ANDERSON Minister of Birnie) who died on the 24TH October 1864 in the 85TH year of her age. And of their second son JAMES, who was born on the 6TH Feb[y]. 1803 and died in 1810.

207. In loving memory of JOHN GRANT and JANE his wife who both died at Orton 1845, 2ND March and 1ST July respectively.

207a. *Broken base, possibly from Stone 207.*

208. Sacred to the memory of JOHN COLLIE, Engineer, Newmill, Iron-works, Elgin, who was accidentally killed at Minmore, Glenlivet, on the 10TH May 1876, aged 21 years. This monument is erected by his Fellow Workmen, as a tribute of esteem.

209. In loving memory of WILLIAM JAMES dearly loved only son of JAMES & JESSIE CLARK, Aulthash, Keith, who died suddenly at Forresterhill 5TH Jan. 1944 aged 17 years. Also his father JAMES FRASER CLARK who died 20TH Feb. 1972 aged 77 years, at Spynie Hospital. And his mother JESSIE DONALDSON who died at Broomhill Cottage, Mosstodloch 22ND Feb. 1979 aged 82 years, dearly beloved wife of the said JAMES F .CLARK and his dear sister JANET ANNE CLARK who died at Broomhill Cottage 11TH Feb. 2001 aged 76 years.

210. In loving memory of WILLIAM CLARK, beloved husband of ELSIE MILNE who died at Muir of Lochs 7TH Dec. 1932 aged 79 years. Also the

said ELSIE MILNE who died at Aulthash Cottage, Fochabers 28TH Feb. 1947 aged 91 years.

211. In memory of JANET THOMPSON daughter of Captain GEORGE KAY born at Tannachy near Forres in September 1804 and died at Lochhill on 5TH January 1892. To die is gain. Erected by her nephews JAMES and JOHN GRAY in Ontario, Canada.

212. Erected by ALEXANDER TAYLOR, Farmer in Clockeasy, in memory of his son JAMES TAYLOR, who died the 14th April 1835 aged 20 years. The above mentioned ALEXANDER TAYLOR, died 22nd June 1850 aged 77 years. Also his spouse ISABELLA JENKINS, who died 23rd May 1859, aged 81 years.

213. In memory of JOHN TAYLOR, North Darkland, who died 9TH Augt. 1888 aged 48 years. And of his wife MARGARET PYPER, who died at North Darkland, 24TH May 1913, aged 60 years. Also the wife of their son ALEXANDER, ISOBEL BEGG, M.B.E., who died at Boat of Garten 11TH April 1965, aged 79 years. And the above ALEXANDER, who died 12TH August 1965, aged 79 years.

214. Erected in memory of ALEXANDER GRANT, late Forester, Innes House, who departed this life the 13th Septr. 1849, aged 72 years. He was for 50 years in the Service of the late JAMES, EARL of FIFE.

215. In loving memory of JOHN TAYLOR Crofter, Urquhart, who died at Urquhart 26TH Feb. 1903 aged 60 years, also of his wife ANN GRANT who died at Urquhart 9TH April 1926 aged 78 years, and their daughters, JANE who died at Lhanbryde 7TH July 1895 aged 25 years. ELSIE who died at Urquhart 14TH Dec. 1905 aged 22 years. ISABELLA who died at Rothes 29TH Dec. 1908 aged 28 years. ANN DUNCAN who died at Fife-Keith, 6TH Sept. 1921 aged 53 years. And their sons, JAMES who died at Las Cruces, Mexico, 9TH April 1912 aged 47 years. WILLIAM who died at Stockton, U.S.A., 7TH Nov. 1914 aged 42 years. HUGH GRANT died at San Rafail, Cal: 4TH July 1932 aged 58 years. ROBERT died at Lhanbryde 29TH Jan.1942 aged 52 years. Also their daughters, JESSIE died at Jointurelands 2ND June 1954 aged 87 years. ELIZABETH died at Foresterhill, Aberdeen 24TH Dec. 1954 aged 67 years. JOHN died at Merced, U.S.A. 14TH Dec. 1958 aged 82 years. ALEXANDER died at North Shields 25TH March 1970 aged 90 years.

216. Erected by WILLIAM BRANDER, Farmer in Ferniefield, and his brothers ALEXANDER, GEORGE, ROBERT and ANDREW, in memory of their parents, JAMES BRANDER, Farmer in Finfan who died there 15th Feby. 1828 aged 82 years. Also JANNET TAYLOR his spouse who died 6 November 1850 aged 77 years. And their brother JAMES who died 16th October 1826 aged 22 years. (*Punctuation not as on stone, amended for readability.*)

217. To the memory of JOHN REID, late Farmer in Fernafield, (*sic*) who died March 7th 1800 aged 47 years. And JANE GEDDIE his spouse who died 14th

Feby. 1805 aged 50 years. Erected by ALEX^R. REID their son, Wright in Kingstown (*sic*) 1827.

218. Erected by ELIZABETH GILL, in memory of her husband JAMES REID, Inn Keeper, Rothes, who died the 14th day of March 1846, aged 54 years.

219. Erected by the family in loving memory of their father & mother, GEORGE SIMON, Tailor, Meft, died 28TH Dec. 1891 aged 82 years, and JANE WINCHESTER his wife died 17TH Feb. 1895 aged 76 years. Also their brothers & sisters, WILLIAM, died 24TH April 1866, aged 27 years. ALEXANDER, died 21ST July 1866, aged 24 years. ISABELLA, died 1ST Nov. 1871, aged 24 years. MARGARET, died 13TH Feb. 1855, aged 2 years. LOUISA, died 22ND March 1858, aged 6 days. Death is swallowed up in victory.
(*Mason, W.T. Hendry, Elgin.*)

220. Erected to perpetuate the memory of WILLIAM SIMON, Farmer in Nether-meft, who died 17th September 1849 aged 75 years. And his beloved spouse, JEAN BROWN, who died 1st August, 1844 aged 74 years. And their son ALEXANDER SIMON, who died 24th September, 1846 aged 45 years.

221. Erected by JOHN SIMON, Farmer, Meft, in memory of JANE his daughter who died 2ND May 1869 aged 14 years. The said JOHN SIMON who died at Muriehall aged 82 years. His wife MARGARET GRIGOR who died at Elgin, also JOHN SIMON the beloved husband of ANN DEAN who died 24TH Aug. 1917 aged 68 years. Also the above ANN DEAN who died at Tippertait 10TH May 1936 aged 85 years. Also ANNIE DEAN who died at Elgin 21ST May 1990 aged 87 years.

222. Erected by JOSEPH SIMON, in memory of his beloved wife ISABELLA DUNCAN, who died the 11th April 1852, aged 35 years. Also their daughter JANE, who died the 2nd May 1852, aged 10 years. And their daughter ISABELLA who died in July 1852, aged 5 years. WILLIAM SIMON, who died at Elgin, 24th Dec. 1912, aged 66 years.
(*Mason, Hendry, Elgin.*)

222a *Mason's Block.*
J. S.

222b *Mason's Block.*
J.S.

223. In loving memory of MARGARET GRANT who died 5TH Sep. 1937 aged 79 years.

224. Erected to the memory of WILLIAM SHAND who died at Longhill on the 26TH Octr. 183?9, aged 29 years. Also his wife ISABELLA DUNCAN who died 8TH Sep^t. 1893 aged 82 years. Also CHRISTINA WATSON aged 86. Blessed are the dead who die in the Lord.

225 To perpetuate the memory of WILLIAM LITTLEJOHN, Farmer, Luchars (*sic*) who died the 30th of December 1847 aged 86 years. And his spouse JANE HARROLD who died the 26th of January 1852 aged 85 years.

225a. In loving memory of JAN HAPEL died 29TH March 1986 aged 72.

226. In memory of W[M] MacD. INNES, who died 25TH June 1936 aged 80. His son W[M]. B. INNES killed in action 22ND Feb. 1917. His daughter ANNIE J. wife of J. PEARSON, died in U.S.A. 9TH May 1932. His son GEORGE died in infancy. His wife MARGARET DENOON who died 28TH March 1939 aged 81. Their daughter ISABELLA who died 18TH Sep[t]. 1941 aged 49. Their son JOHN who died suddenly at Denny, 24TH Jan. 1948 aged 48. Their daughter MARGARET who died 18TH Oct. 1955 aged 72. Their daughter HELEN died 22ND Dec. 1967 aged 82.
(*Mason, J.R. Henderson.*)

227. In loving memory of HELEN MacKENZIE wife of ALEXANDER MURDOCH who died at Tippertait 15TH April 1946, also the said ALEXANDER MURDOCH who died 19TH April 1958.

228. Sacred to the memory of JOHN REID, sometime Postmaster at Buckie, who died 12th Nov[r]. 1846, aged 59 years. Also of ANN SUTHERLAND, his wife, who died at Post-Office of Buckie, 28th Oct[r]. 1847, aged 62 years. Also of his son, The Rev[d] COSMO REID, who died at Gladhll 5th June 1851, aged 35 years. And of MARGARET, daughter of, & successor to her Father, as Postmistress at Buckie, who died there 3rd Nov[r]. 1855, aged 41 years. This tablet is erected by his only surviving child ANN, & his son-in-law ALEX[R]. HENDRY, Postmaster of Buckie.

229. Sacred to the memory of COSMO REID, late Farmer in Entryhead of Innes, who departed this life on the 23rd Feb[y]. 1832 aged 75 years. Also MARGARET ROBERTSON, his spouse who died the 10th August 1842 aged 88 years.

230. 1855. Sacred to the memory of JAMES REID, late Farmer in Loch-hill, who died 23rd August 1854 aged 78 years. Also of his wife, ISABELLA FORSYTH, who died 22nd March 1875, aged 93 years. This stone is placed here by his two sons ANDREW & ALEXANDER.
(*Mason, Cumming & Young.*)

231. Erected to the memory of ALEXANDER REID late Farmer, Loch-hill, who died 27TH December 1871 aged 55 years. Also of his son, JAMES, who died at Hoste Island, Cape Horn 1876, aged 24 years. His wife ELIZABETH DUNCAN died 5TH Jan[y]. 1889.

232. In memory of CHRISTINA MUNRO, who died upon the 28th Aug[t]. 1844 aged 61. She was for many years an attached & faithful Servant in the family of the Rev[d]. ALEX[R]. WALKER, Minister of this Parish, whose two youngest sons have erected this stone as a mark of their esteem.

233. 1908. Sacred to the memory of JEMIMA BRANDER, wife of JOHN REID, who died at Lochhill, 9TH July 1905, aged 56 years. Also their daughter ELIZABETH REID, who died 10TH Feby. 1887 aged 8 years.

234. *Walled enclosure with five tablets on walls.*

234a. HENRY WALKER Captain & Adjutant of the Inverne*f*s Shire Militia, died 2nd Jany. 1845 aged 61. Here also in the same grave are interred the remains of his wife WILLIAMINA CHALMERS who died at ... on the 30th ... 18(*4*)9, *remainder illegible.*

234b. The Reverend HENRY WALKER Minister of Ordiquhill, was called to succeed his father as Minister of Urquhart 18th May 1847: and died at Urquhart 20th June 1859, in the 38th year of his age, and the 16th of his Ministry.

234c. Here are interred the remains of JOHN CRUICKSHANK Esqr. late Surgeon in the service of the Honb^{le} East India Company at S^t. Helena, who died at Springfield, near Elgin on the 22^d day of Octb^r. 1815 in the 34th year of his age, a man highly esteemed for his professional abilities and exemplary in his moral and religious conduct. This monument was erected to his memory by his affectionate widow M^{RS} ELIZA GREENTREE daughter of Colonel GREENTREE of Fairy Land in the Island of S^t. Helena. Their son TH^{OS}. GREENTREE CRUICKSHANK who died in his infancy at Banff on the 27th day of May 1816, is also interred here.

234d. (*Top part missing*)
Here lie the remains of Rev. ALEX. WALKER, Minister of this Parish from (1811-1825) (1841-1847), born 1778, died 1847, and his wife ELIZABETH GRANT DUFF of Eden died 1855.

234e. This tablet is erected to the memory of the Rev^d. ALEXANDER WALKER, who was ordained to the Parish of Old Machar in 1805, translated to Urquhart in 1811, to Elgin in 1825, and re-translated to Urquhart in 1841, where he died. Honored (*sic*) and lamented on the 28th January, 1847, in the 69th year of his age and the 42nd of his Ministry. His remains are interred in the parish burial ground.

235a. 1883. Erected by ANN ARCHIBALD in memory of her husband ALEXANDER CHRISTIE who died 22nd March 1882 aged 65 years. Also of his wife ANN ARCHIBALD who died at Findrassie in May 1899.

235b. Erected by JAMES MAIR, Farmer, Innes in memory of his beloved wife MARGARET WESTLAND who died at Innes on the 20th of February 1882 aged 49 years. Also the said JAMES MAIR, who died at Glencairn, Baltimore, U.S.America, 5th July 1883, aged 52 years, and his daughter MAGGIE ANN MAIR, the beloved wife of the JOHN M^{c}DONALD, Tailor, Elgin, who died 2nd Octr. 1883 aged 24 years.

235c. Erected by ALEXANDER MITCHELL, Skene in memory of his beloved wife JESSIE M^cBAIN MAIR, who died the 10th of July 1880 aged 24 years. Also their son WILLIAM who died the 8th of September 1879 aged 12 weeks.

236. To the very dear memory of JANE ELIZA DONALD STUART INGRAM whose great talents and innocent life death suddenly quenched at Aberdeen on 9th Decr. 1899 when she was only 22 years old. And of JOHN KYD GORDON INGRAM, who in youth early disclosed a nature that was as wise and manly as it was generous and pure. He sleeps at Colombo where he died on 5th Feby. 1902 in his 26th year.

237. In loving memory of M^{RS}. MARGARET ROSS KYD wife of the Rev^d. GORDON INGRAM, Minister of Urquhart who died there 4th August 1882 aged 37 years. Also of JANE ELIZA DONALD, their infant daughter, who died on the 9th July 1873, and of ANNE GORDON their second daughter who died on the 15th August 1884, aged 17 years. And of MARGARET ANNE STEPHEN their eldest daughter, who died on the 27th September 1886 aged 22 years. The said Rev^d. GORDON INGRAM, who is commemorated in the Church.
In loving memory of JOHANNA DURRAN INGRAM, who died at Edinburgh on 6th July 1903 aged 89 years. Farewell sweet sister.

238. Sacred to the memory of CHARLES PHYN late Farmer in Darkland, who died 1st March 1845 aged 83 years. Also his son ALEXANDER who died 10th May 1847 aged 47 years. Also JANE PHYN daughter of JOHN PHYN, Farmer, Darkland who died 11th July 1856, aged 5 years. Also JANE TOD, wife of said CHARLES PHYN who died 15th February 1859, aged 85 years. Also ISABELLA GRIGOR, wife of said JOHN PHYN, who died 9th February 1861 aged 37 years. Also said JOHN PHYN who died 24th August 1887, aged 83 years.

239. Erected to the memory of JOHN CRUICKSHANK, sometime Farmer in Coxton, who died at Urquhart 13th May 1897 aged 84. And of his widow AGNES PHYN who died at Urquhart 15th Sep^t. 1903 aged 87.

239a. *Mason's Block.*
?   B N.?

239b. *Mason's Block.*
Illegible.

240. Erected by ALEXANDER BRANDER, Farmer, Lochs, in loving memory of his son JAMES A. BRANDER, who died on the 16TH Decr. 1915, aged 23 years. Also the said ALEXANDER BRANDER who died at Lochs, 30TH April 1923 in his 82ND year. And his wife JANE GERRIE who died at Lochs 10TH Oct. 1924 aged 73 years. And their daughter ANNIE who died 18TH Nov. 1963 aged 84 years. Also their daughter MARGARET who died 6TH March 1974 aged 87 years. Sadly missed.

241. Sacred to the memory of PETER BROWN, Shipmaster, who died on board the Barque, Northern Chief, of Lossiemouth, Nov. 4TH 1876 aged 28 years, and is interred here.

242. In memory of JOHN BROWN, late Farmer at Corbiewell, died at Urquhart March 18th 1898 aged 84 years. Also his wife ELSPET PHIMISTER, who died Jany. 22nd 1901, aged 82 years. Also their son JOHN BROWN who died at Launceston, Tasmania, 10th Decr. 1918 aged 61 years. And of their daughters, ISABELLA born 5th June 1846, died 16th June 1937. ELSPET born 2nd Octr. 1854, died 27th Feby. 1938. Also their son ALEXANDER who died in Durban 13th August 1938 aged 79 years. MARY ANN born 20th August 1850, died 26th May 1941 and ELIZA born 26th Decr. 1862, died 24th Jany. 1944.

243. Sacred to the memory of JAMES P. BROWN, Farmer, Dipple, born at Innesmill 12TH Feb. 1870 died 15TH Dec. 1936 and of his wife LIZZIE REID died 1ST March 1953 aged 81 years, also their elder daughter ISABELLA, died 3RD March 1985 aged 84 years, and their daughter AGNES CHRISTIAN died 3RD Nov. 1997 aged 95 years.

244. *Stone marked on 1978 plan but no inscription recorded in 1978 survey, no stone now visible.*

245. *West Face.*
Erected by JOHN BROWN, Farmer, Innes Mill, in memory of his son JOSEPH REID, who died 4TH Aug. 1875, aged 6 years.
South face.
Also ISABELLA REID, his wife who died 23RD March 1876, aged 30 years. And his daughter ISABELLA who died 21st Aug. 1876, aged 6 months. "Be ye therefore ready also."
East Face.
The said JOHN BROWN died at Peebles 7TH March 1909, aged 77 years. And his son JOHN NICOL died at Eastbourne 29TH April 1922 aged 50 years. Also his daughter ANNIE wife of G.U. MACDONALD died at Peebles 6TH Dec. 1939.

246. 1868. In memory of WILLIAM HOSSACK, Carpenter, who died April 1848, aged 41 years, and of his wife ELIZABETH MUSTARD, who died 6TH May 1864, aged 53 years. Also of their son JOHN who died February 1847 aged 11 years, and WILLIAM, who died 15TH April 1862, aged 24 years and of ELIZABETH who was interred at Birnie aged 2 years.
(*Mason, Goodwillie.*)

247. Erected by ELSPET ALLAN in memory of her husband ALEXANDER RAMSAY, who died at Finfan-wells 20TH December 1880 aged 75 years, and the said ELSPET ALLAN who died 18TH March 1892 aged 80 years.

248. *Flat stone.*

In memory of ANNE MARGARET BENTON wife of WILLIAM BENTON, only daughter of WILLIAM and ANNE MARGARET STEPHEN died at Send Surrey, on 15TH November 1931 aged 86.

249. Erected by ISABELLA CATTANACH, in memory of her brother and sisters, JANET CATTANACH, who died at Harestones, on the 8TH February 1874, aged 74 years, and of GEORGE CATTANACH, who died at Harestones, on the 11TH March 1877, aged 63 years. Also of ANN CATTANACH who died at Troves, on the 14TH January 1880, aged 73 years, and of JAMES CATTANACH, late Farmer, Harestones, who died at Troves on the 24TH August 1881, aged 79 years. Also ISABELLA CATTANACH, who died at Harestones 29TH April 1877, aged 11 years. And ISABELLA CATTANACH, late of Harestones, who died at Elgin 24TH August 1886, aged 70 years. (*Mason, T. Goodwillie.*)

250. In loving memory of JAMES MUSTARD, Pittensair, Lhanbryde, who died 21ST June 1926 aged 64 years. Also his wife BERTHA who died 7TH April 1951 aged 85 years. Erected by his widow.

251. In memoriam, JAMES MUSTARD, Unthank, 1819-1913. His wife JESSIE RHIND, 1819-1896. Their family, WILLIAM 1857-1885. ROBERT 1855-1902. Also their daughter ELIZABETH, widow of JAMES MUNRO, 1855-1948. MARGARET 1859-1950.

252. In memory of BARBARA DUNCAN who died 8. Jan. 1864 aged 33 years. And her husband GEORGE PHIMISTER who died 8. Jan. 1902 aged 72 years. And their son WILLIAM ALEXANDER, Master Mariner, who died at Garmouth, 3RD Aug. 1909 aged 47 years.

253. Erected to the memory of MARGRET (*sic*) ANDERSON, spouse to MICHEL (*sic*) PHIMISTER, Farmer in Corbiewell, who died 28th Feby. 1838 aged 81 years. This stone is placed here by her sons (*sic*) WILLIAM PHIMISTER, who died 21st May 1880, aged 86.

254. Erected to the memory of MICHEL (*sic*) PHIMISTER late Farmer in Corbiewell, who died 3rd Novr. 1840 aged 83 years. This stone is placed here by his sons JAMES PHIMISTER who died 30th December 1854, aged 66 years. And ISABELLA PHIMISTER, who died 4th April 1868 aged 83 years.

255. In loving memory of my dear husband WILLIAM BROWN who died at Bogs of Leuchars 1ST Sep. 1936. Also his wife ELLA SOUTER WYLLIE who died 14TH April 1963. MARGARET REID MOORE nee BROWN 1927 – 1983. JESSIE (JANET) PHIMISTER BROWN 1918 – 2000. *Flower holder.* B.

256. *Flat stone.*
1859. Sacred to the memory of JOHN, who died 16 February 1816, and of CATHERINE JANE, who died 22nd January 1856 aged fourteen months, also of MARY ANN, who died 22nd July 1858 aged eight years, children of JOHN ALEXANDER COOPER, Merchant in Elgin, and of ANN STEPHEN, his

spouse and of the said JOHN ALEXANDER COOPER, who died at Spynie 1st June 1881 aged 66 years. And of the said ANN STEPHEN wife of the above JOHN A. COOPER and daughter of the late JAMES STEPHEN Esq., Old Keith, she departed this life at N° 8 The College, Glasgow, 24th February 1909 aged 96 years.
"I look for the Resurrection of the (*dead*) and the life of the world to come."

256a. *Mason's Block.*
W. C.

257. *Pillared Cross on a base of three circular steps.*
Top section.
Beneath this cross the sign of the common salvation rest in hope of a blessed resurrection.
The bodies of the Rev. JAMES COOPER, A.M. Schoolmaster of Urquhart, who died 1839, of his wife ANNE REID who died 1856 and of their unmarried daughters ANNE, who died 1812 and MARY who died at Elgin 1892, also of their second son JOHN ALEXANDER COOPER who died at Spynie 1881 aged 67, his wife ANN STEPHEN who died at Glasgow College 1909 aged 96 and of their children who died young, JOHN, CATHERINE JANE and MARY ANN. Their son ALEXANDER COOPER died at Perth, Western Australia 1911 aged 64.
Middle section.
Here also rests in the same blessed hope the mortal body of JAMES COOPER son of JOHN ALEXANDER COOPER born in Elgin February 13, 1846, died in Elgin December Minister at ST Stephens, Broughty-Ferry 1873-1881, at The East Church of ST. Nicholas, Aberdeen 1881, Professor of Ecclesiastical History in the University of Glasgow 1898-1922, Moderator of the General Assembly.
Base section.
"Lord I have loved the habitation of thy House, and the place where thine honour dwelleth."

258. *Flat stone.*
Sacred to the memory of The Rev. JAMES COOPER sometime Schoolmaster of this parish who died at Urquhart on 5th October 1839, aged 67. Also of ANNE REID his spouse who died at Elgin, on 30th January 1856 aged 78. And of MARY their eldest child who died unmarried at Elgin the 17th day of February 1892 in the 85th year of her age. Beneath this stone lie the remains of JAMES COOPER D.D. And of his widow MARGARET WILLIAMSON who died 17th May 1947 and of JOSEPHINE WILLIAMSON sister of the said MARGARET WILLIAMSON who died 1st November 1950. "The generation of the upright shall be blessed."

259. In loving memory of JAMES ROUGH, for 48 years Gamekeeper on the Innes Estate, who died at Bishopmill, on 25TH May 1907 aged 77 years. And of ELIZABETH BROWN, his wife who died at Elginshill on 4TH Sep. 1889 aged 52 years.

260. In loving memory of ALEXANDER SHAND who died at Woodpark 3RD May 1914 aged 79. His son ALEXANDER died 3RD March 1915 aged 50. And his son WILLIAM died in infancy, interred in Alvah Churchyard. Also his wife ISABELLA DAVIDSON, died 26TH August 1919 aged 80.

261. In memory of GEORGE HENDRY, Crofter, Muir of Lochs, died 9TH October 1904, aged 72 years. And his wife CATHERINE GRANT, died 31ST December 1915, aged 86 years.

262. In memory of ALEXANDER GILLIES, who was killed on duty at The Great North Station, Elgin, on the 1ST March 1886, aged 26 years. And also his beloved wife, MARY HENDRY, who died at Urquhart 22ND Novr. 1888 aged 31 years. Erected by his fellow servants.

263. In loving memory of CHARLOTTE MANSON FRENCH beloved wife of WALTER GRANT, who died at Connagedale, Garmouth 22ND Dec. 1943 aged 75 years. Dearly loved & sadly mourned. Also their sons, Pte. JAMES GRANT 31ST Canadians, killed in action on the Somme, 27TH Sep. 1916 aged 24 years. WALTER ALEXANDER died in infancy. Also the said WALTER GRANT who died 2ND Feb. 1951 aged 78 years. And WILLIAM, son of WILLIAM & JESSIE GRANT, died 21ST Feb. 1949.

264. Erected by MARY ASHER in memory of her husband WALTER GRANT, who died April 7TH 1888, aged 41 years. And of the said MARY ASHER who died Jany. 6TH 1928. Deeply mourned. Also of their son WILLIAM, Baker & Confectioner, 35 High Street, Elgin, who died there May 12TH 1937. Deeply mourned. And their grandchildren, ELMA ASHER SHAW 1917-1970. JAMES A.D. SHAW, Edinvillie, Moray, died Jan. 23RD 2000, aged 80 years, dear father of JUDITH & MARK and beloved husband of MURIEL SCOTT died Jan. 3RD 2004 aged 84, beloved mother and grandmother.

265. In loving memory of ELIZABETH GRANT, dearly loved wife of ALEXANDER GORDON who died at 35 High S^t., Elgin, 4TH July 1960. Also the said ALEXANDER GORDON, who died 7TH Sep. 1964.

266. Erected by JOHN M^{c}LEAN in memory of his parents JOHN M^{c}LEAN, who died 13TH Jany. 1865 aged 48 years. And MARGARET PEDDIE, who died 30TH April 1872 aged 56 years.

267. Erected by ANDREW FORSYTH, Lochs of Urquhart, in memory of his daughter MARGARET, who died 6TH Octr. 1875 aged 24 years. Also the said ANDREW FORSYTH, who died 6TH April 1884 aged 62 years. His daughter ISABELLA, who died 28TH July 1937 aged 90 years. And her husband CHARLES EDDIE, a native of Brechin who died 24TH Nov. 1957 aged 82 years.

268 – 268c are tablets in fragment of wall, possibly part of the old church wall. The parts of the inscriptions in parenthesis are taken from PSAS 1966-67, Vol C pp253-254.

268   IN SPEM B. RESURRECTIONIS Requiescit vir Reverendus et Eruditus Mr. ALEXR. GADDERAR Paroeciae de Girvan, cui Prae fuit ad annum 1688. Ecclesiae et Regno Scotiae antiquissimis faustum, in Diocesi Glascuensi Pastor Canonice Ordinatus, Cum ille, una cum trecentis circiter aliis, sacris ordinibus Regniq. Legibus unitis, contra jura omnia divina humanaq. Tumultuant ibus in Apostolicum Ecclesiae Regimen Conjuratis Gregem et Reditum vi armata amittere esset coactus. Tandem rediit in Comitatum hunc Moraviesem natale ((Solum ubi Praedicationi Dei verbi administrationi S. Sacra mentorum necnon Cultui Divino ut obtinet in Ecclesia Anglicana seipsum feliciter dedit.)) Propriis sum ptibus Populo ut prodesset S. Ministerio fungebatur. Erat filius natu Maximus GIULIELMI GADDERAR viri inclytae probitatis ex Antiqua Familia de COWFORD ( )m ex Conjuge MARGARETA MARSHAL Haerede agrorum in Ditione Urquhartensi ex avitis Patribus sibi devenientium. Supersunt illi ex Imo Matrimonio cum CATHARINA LAMY filia Antiquae Familiae Dunkenny in Angusia Filius Unigenitus IOANNES GADDERAR A.M. Londini Chirurgo Medicus Et duae filiae ANNA et ISOBELLA ex 2do Matrimonio cum ANNA COOK Moraviensi susceptae.

Obiit XX1X Quintil. Anno Dominicae Incarnationis MDCCX1V aetat. suae 71 Beatus vir qui suffert tentationem; quoniam cum Probatus fuerit, accipiet Coronam vitae, quam repromisit Deus diligentibus. Jac 1, X11

Translation taken from PSAS 1966-67, Vol C pp253-254.
In the hope of the blessed Resurrection rests a Reverend and learned man Mr. ALEXANDER GADDERAR of the Parish of Girvan of which he was in charge until 1688, a year propitious to the most ancient church and realm of Scotland, in the diocese of Glasgow. A canonically ordained priest when he with some three hundred others was forced by armed might to forfeit flock and living as the holy ordinances and statutes of the Kingdom, uniting in a rebellion contrary to the laws of God and man, had conspired against the Apostolic Rule of the Church. At length he returned to this county of Moray, his native land, where he cheerfully gave himself up to preaching the word of God, administering the Holy Sacraments and to the form of divine worship obtaining in the Anglican Church. At his own expense, he performed his Holy duty to benefit the people. He was the eldest son of WILLIAM GADDERAR, a man of notable goodness, from the ancient family of Cowford, by WILLIAM GADDERAR'S wife MARGARET MARSHAL, heiress to lands in the lordship of Urquhart that came to her from her ancestors. From his first marriage with CATHERINE LAMY, daughter of the ancient family of Dunkenny in Angus there survive his only son JOHN GADDERAR A.M. Surgeon and Physician in London, and two daughters ANNA and ISOBELLA from his second marriage with ANNA COOK of Moray. He died 29TH of July in the year of our lord's Incarnation 1714 aged 71.

268a.   In memoriam WILLIAM STEPHEN F.R.C.S.L. of West Cults who died at Fosterseat on the 8TH May 1877, aged 73 years. Also of his son ALEXANDER REID who died at Texas, U.S. on the 22ND December 1878 aged (?) years.

268b. Sacred to the memory of MARGARET BURGES, who died 6th May1822, aged 24 years. In testimony of his sincere regard for his beloved wife, this tablet was placed here by ALEXANDER REID, Easter Elchies. The said ALEXANDER REID died at Easter Elchies, on 18th October 1847, aged 65.

268c. ALEXANDER REID, only son of the said A. REID & M. BURGES, died also at Easter Elchies, on 5TH March 1848, aged 26.

268d. *Flat stone, top part broken.*
....ANN MARGARET STEPHEN daughter of the late ALEXANDER REID died at Easter Elchies 15th May 1856 aged 35 years. .... stone is placed here in memory of his dearly beloved wife *(by)* WILLIAM STEPHEN 1856.

269. *Flat stone.*
Here lyes the body of IAMES REID, Fewer in Urquhart, who died the 1? day of Aprile 1765 & his spouse ANNA GADDERAR who died the 2ND of Septr. 1772. Also of JOHN REID their eldest son, late fewer in Urquhart who died Ser.? 18 1785 and JEAN BARRON his spouse who died 6TH May 1829 aged 86.

270. Erected by WILLIAM HAY, Postmaster, Invernes *(sic)*: son of JEREMIAH HAY of Speymouth, in memory of his son GEORGE who died in infancy 7th July 1822.

271. *Table stone.*
This is the buriab *(sic)* place of JEREMIAH HAY, Farmer in Orblestown who died 18?th Decr. 1823? and MARGARET BROWN his spouse, who died the 3rd March 1830, and their children. Also GEORGE HAY, their second son who died Oct. ?? 1797 aged 23 years & 10 months.
This stone is erected by JAMES HAY (Farmer?) Orblestown, their eldest son in memory of his brother and parents. Also is intered *(sic)* in this place their sons JAMES, JOHN, ALEXANDER and JEREMIAH. Full of brotherly love.
Monogram J H on south panel.

272. Sacred to the memory of GEORGE LEGGE beloved husband of ANN F. LAWRENCE who died 23RD February 1942 aged 71 years. Also the above ANN F. LAWRENCE who died 11TH March 1944 aged 70 years. Sadly missed.

273. How lovely is thy dwelling place *(Winged angel portrait surmounting tablet inscription.)*
Sacred to the memory of HELEN SIMON, who died at Coxton on the 18TH June 1834 aged 25 years. Also of her husband FRANCIS HENDRY, who died at New Field on the 31ST May 1877 aged 72 years. And his remains are interred in another part of this burying-ground. Erected by their family.

274. In loving memory of HELEN MACKINNON born 1926, died at Teesside 1972 beloved wife of WILLIAM J. GREIG.

275. *East face.*
In remembrance of HELEN ROBSON or SINCLAIR who died at Maverston on the 21ST August 1909 aged 74 years. Also her daughter ANN who died at Deans Crook 9TH February 1939 aged 84 years.
South face.
Also of her grand daughter NELLY SINCLAIR or MACKINNON who died 21ST Dec. 1973 aged 85 years, daughter of JAMES & HELEN SINCLAIR.
North face.
Also of her son JAMES SINCLAIR husband of HELEN JOANNA TAYLOR who died at Scotstonhill on the 14TH June 1912 aged 55 years. Also the said HELEN JOANNA TAYLOR who died at Deans Crook on the 30TH July 1937 aged 81 years.
(Mason, Wilson, Elgin.)

275a. In loving memory of ANTHONY (TONY) CUMMINS who died in Edinburgh 8$_{TH}$ December 1994 aged 65, dear husband of EVIE MACKINNON.

276. *Stone marked on 1978 plan but no inscription recorded in 1978 survey, no stone now visible.*

277. In loving memory of WILLIAM CANT, Lawrenceton, Farmer, who died at Speyslaw 22ND July 1895 aged 66, also his daughter JANE ANN CANT who died at Lawrenceton 27TH Sep. 1906 aged 21. And his son JAMES CANT, who died at Lawrenceton 25TH August 1909 aged 25, also his wife JANE ASHER who died at Lawrenceton 9TH Nov. 1947 aged 87, also their son WILLIAM A. CANT, Lawrenceton, Forres who died at Inverness 3RD April 1963 aged 76.

277a. *Mason's Block.*
?. C.

278. In loving memory of MARY STEPHEN wife of JOHN WILLIAMSON who died 28TH Aug. 1939 aged 84 years. Also the said JOHN WILLIAMSON who died 23RD Dec. 1940 aged 85 years. Also their daughter MARY who died 8TH Feb. 1960 aged 79 years.
(Mason, Wilson).

279. In loving memory of MARY ANN SKAKELS, wife of JOHN MORRISON, Blackburn, who died 7TH Feb. 1937 aged 78.

280. Erected by ISABELLA STEWART in loving memory of her husband WILLIAM ALLAN who died at Garmouth 25TH Oct. 1936 aged 81 years. The said ISABELLA STEWART who died 1ST June 1942 aged 67 years.

281. In loving memory of ALEXANDER M^{c}INTOSH, died at Lochhill on 24TH April 1936 aged 78 years, and his wife JANE ROBERTSON died on 11TH May 1936 aged 78 years. Also their sons, JOHN, killed in action 1916 aged 22 years. JAMES, died of wounds 1917 aged 22 years. Erected by the family. M^{c}INTOSH.

282. In loving memory of PETER FALCONER who died at Greenside 16TH
March 1903 aged 74 years. His wife CATHERINE DUNCAN who died 4TH
February 1917 aged 78 years. Their son JAMES who died 30TH January 1916
aged 58 years. Their daughter ELIZABETH who died at Buckie 25TH March
1927 aged 61 years. Their daughter ANNIE who died at Lhanbryde 10TH
Feby. 1931 aged 63 years. Their daughter CATHERINE who died at
Lhanbryde 11TH July 1961 aged 82 years.
Their grandchild ELIZA who died 8TH April 1886 aged 5 years.

283. In loving remembrance of WILLIAM MONRO, born at Grange 13TH July
1836, died at Urquhart 9TH March 1891, also his wife MARGARET ALLAN,
born 23RD July 1836, died 26TH Sep. 1927. And their son JOHN, born 1ST Oct.
1862, died 2ND Sep. 1925, also their daughter JANE, born 28TH March 1875,
died 20TH Jan. 1926, who both died in U.S.A.
Erected by his widow and family.

284. 1853. Erected to the memory of JANET BUIE, who died at Urquhart, 16th
May 1851, aged 21 years. This stone is placed here by her beloved brother
DONALD, at S^t. Louis, United States of America, as a last token of esteem
for his departed sister. His brother PETER aged 9 years, ALEXANDER aged
7 years, who both died 27th Feb. 1827, and JAMES who died 23rd March
1834 aged 1 year, and are interred in the Elgin Cathedral.

285. *Obelisk.*
East face.
Erected by GEORGE & W^M. DUNCAN in memory of their parents &^{c} viz.
GEORGE DUNCAN, who died at Kingston, the 11TH day of August 1857,
aged 85 years. ANN DUNCAN, his spouse who died 26TH Decr. 1841, aged
69.
North face.
Also of GEORGE DUNCAN son of the said W^M DUNCAN, who died 18TH
Sep^{tr}. 1856 aged 10 years. In affectionate remembrance of HELEN ALLAN,
the dearly beloved wife of WILLIAM DUNCAN, who fell asleep in Jesus
October 14TH 1883, aged 75 years. Also the said WILLIAM DUNCAN who
died at Sea-view Place, Buckie, March 30TH 1890, aged 80 years.
South face.
And ANNIE DUNCAN, daughter of WILLIAM DUNCAN who died at Sea-
view Place, Buckie, 30TH April 1901 aged 59 years. Also HELEN DUNCAN
(daughter) who died February 12TH 1923 aged 82 years.

286. In loving memory of JESSIE K. ROBERTSON wife of GEORGE GRAY
died at Redbog 18TH March 1935, also her sister MARJORY F.
ROBERTSON wife of JAMES MELVIN died at Errol Cottage, Lhanbryde,
15TH March 1939, also her sister ISABELLA J. ROBERTSON died 16TH
March 1955.

287. In loving memory of CLARA INGLEFIELD beloved wife of GEORGE
MITCHELL who died at Florida Villa 4TH June 1943 aged 78 years. Dearly

loved and sadly mourned. Also in loving memory of GEORGE MITCHELL who died on 27TH May 1957 aged 86 years. MITCHELL.

288. Erected in memory of JOHN JAMIESON who died at Burnside, Kingston 10TH December 1946 aged 67 years. JAMIESON.

289. Erected to the memory of ALEXANDER MACKID, Hillockhead, who died 21st March 1817, aged 84 and his spouse ANN ROSS who died 21st March 1820 aged 89. As a tribute of filial respect by their son JOHN MACKID, Mains of Wattin.

290. In loving memory of WILLIAM WEBSTER who died 28TH Nov. 1951 aged 69 years. Also his wife MAGGIE LOGIE who died 22ND Dec. 1966 aged 82 years.
(*Mason, Wilson.*)

291. In loving memory of ALEXANDER BREMNER died 22ND Nov. 1916 aged 76, and his wife JESSIE M^{c}DONALD died 14TH Sep. 1928 aged 88. Also his grandson ALEXANDER BREMNER died of wounds received in France 27TH July 1916 aged 27. And his only son ALEXANDER BREMNER who died in Australia 5TH July 1920 aged 56.

292. Erected by JOHN FORSYTH, Urquhart, in memory of his sons, ALEXANDER who died at Corfue 25th May 1844, aged 22. And COLLING (*sic*) who died at Urquhart 26th November 1846, aged 17 years. The said JOHN FORSYTH, a beloved father and a most dutiful husband died at Urquhart on the 14th October 1855, aged 80 years. And this inscription is placed here by his sorrowing widow to perpetuate the memory of her affectionate husband. Also in memoriam of HELEN YOUNG, beloved wife of the said JOHN FORSYTH who died at Govan, 24th Novr. 1868, aged 81 years, and is interred in the Southern Necropolis, Glasgow.

293. Erected by ALEXANDER & ELIZA MACKENZIE in memory of their beloved daughter ISOBEL who died at West Maverston 1ST March 1942 aged 25 years. Also our beloved son NORMAN who was accidentally killed 17TH June 1950 aged 34 years. Also our dear daughter JEAN beloved wife of ROBERT M^{c}COOKIN who died 4TH January 1955 aged 35 years. Also the said ELIZA MACKENZIE who died 28TH February 1957 aged 77 years. Also the said ALEXANDER MACKENZIE who died 19TH Feb. 1976 aged 94 years.

294. Erected by ELSPET MILNE in memory of her beloved husband GEORGE EDWARD ANDERSON who died at Hills, 26TH May 1877, aged 62 years. Also of their son GEORGE, who died 3RD April 1852. Also ELSPET ANDERSON (widow) died 20TH May 1915, aged 87 years.
(*Mason, T. Goodwillie.*)

295. Sacred to the memory of children of GEORGE HENDRY who died at Woodpark, in childhood. And of ROBERT R. HENDRY who died at Elgin in 1882, aged 18 years. Also the said GEORGE HENDRY who died at Elgin in

1898, aged 66 years. And of BARBARA REID his wife who died at Elgin in 1912, aged 83 years.
Replaced by surviving children 1919.

296. 1855. Erected by ALEXANDER GOW, Farmer, Milltown of Pluscarden, in memory of his father, ROBERT GOW, late Farmer their (*sic*), who died on the 9TH March 1851, aged 76 years. Also of his daughters, viz, MARGRET, who died in infancy, ELSPET who died the 18TH Nov. 1852, aged 18 years. (*Mason, W^M. Taylor, Scul^r., Elgin.*)

297. Erected by MARGARET REID, in memory of her beloved husband ANDREW FORSYTH, Farmer, late of Brandston, who died at Lhanbryde, 24TH Novr. 1898 aged 88 years. And of the said MARGARET REID, who died 8TH Novr. 1902 aged 81 years.
Blessed are the peacemakers; for they shall be called the children of God.

298. Erected by ANDREW FORSYTH, Farmer, Brandston, in memory of his mother, MARGARET HAY, who died at Urquhart, on the 7TH day of March 1858, aged 68 years.
(*Mason, T. Goodwillie.*)

298a. *Mason's Block.*
T. W.

299. *Celtic Cross.*
In memory of SARAH SINCLAIR born at the Island of Eigg, 6TH March 1866 died 1ST April 1934, and of her brother, the REV. PATRICK SINCLAIR D.S.O. the revered and beloved Minister of this Parish for forty three years, born 16TH March 1868 died at Edinburgh 3RD January 1952 and laid to rest there.

300. In loving memory of JOHN WILLIAM DENOON, Draper, Carlinebeg, Lossiemouth, who died 9TH December 1935 aged 66 years, and his wife AGNES BARBARA REID, daughter of JAMES REID, Maverston, who died 3RD November 1957 aged 89 years.
(*Mason, J.R. Henderson, Elgin.*)

301. In loving memory of Lieut. JOHN B. REID 6TH Seaforth Hrs. dearly beloved second son of ALEXANDER & JEMIMA REID, Gladhill, who died of wounds received in action at Madagascar, 12TH May 1942 aged 23 years. "Ever Remembered." Also the said ALEXANDER REID who died 7TH Feb. 1950 aged 63 years. And the said JEMIMA REID who died 29TH May 1950 aged 61 years. Also J.E. MARY REID died Lamont, Canada, 12TH July 1992, aged 66 years.

301a. *Small heart shaped stone in front of 301.*
In loving memory of CAROLYN MARY infant daughter of GRAHAM & GLADYS REID, Gladhill, April 1953.

302. In loving memory of ISABELLA RHIND, daughter of JAMES RHIND, Saddler, Lhanbryde, born 26TH August 1841, died 11TH September 1895 aged 54 years.

303. 1896. Erected by ANDREW & JANE MILNE in loving memory of their son JAMES, who died at Urquhart 4TH May 1885, aged 20 years. And their children, ISABELLA & JOHN, who died in infancy. Parted on earth together in heaven.
(Mason, W.T. Hendry, Elgin.)

304. Erected by JAMES WATSON in memory of his father WILLIAM WATSON who died at Moss of Meft 9th March 1858 aged 80 years. Also of his brother JOHN WATSON who died at Newmill, 8TH Sep^{t}. 1858 aged 50 years

305. Erected by JOHN CRAMOND in memory of his beloved son, ROBERT, who died at Lochhillmoor, on the 12th June 1864, aged 15 years, JOHN CRAMOND 1818-1896, ELLEN BUIE or CRAMOND 1810-1899.

306. In memory of GEORGE WHITE, who died 28TH March 1869, aged 82 years. His wife ANNE DUNCAN, died 17TH April 1880, aged 84 years. And of their family JOHN, JAMES & JANNET. The above all died at Urquhart, and are interred here. ANNIE & ELSIE (Mrs HIRD) died at Edinburgh, and are interred in the Dean Cemetery there. ALEXANDER, died at Chicago, U.S.A. 14TH Oct^{r}.1900. GEORGE, died at Hamilton, Canada, 14TH June 1905. WILLIAM, died at Honolulu, Hawiian Islands, 18TH April 1907.
(Mason, W.T. Hendry, Elgin.)

306a. *Mason's Block, facing south.*
J. F.

307. In loving memory of ALFRED G. GEILS, Innesmill, died 22ND March 1937 aged 40. And GEORGE GEILS retired Farmer late of Innesmill died 30TH Nov. 1948 aged 88, and his wife MARIA HUTCHESON died 14TH Oct. 1955 aged 87. Also LIZZIE HUTCHESON died 4TH May 1976, niece of MARIA HUTCHESON and beloved wife of the late JAMES LESLIE HARDIE, Doohill, Lhanbryde.
(Mason, J.R. Henderson.)

308. Sacred to the memory of MARGARET DUNCAN, Greens of Coxton who died at Elgin, 4th August 1818 aged 52 years. This stone is placed here by ELISABETH DUNCAN as a tribute of respect to her deeply regretted sister.

308a. GEORGE STEWART died at Urquhart 8TH Aug. 1913 aged 63, also his wife ISABELLA M^{AC}INTOSH, died 11TH Sep. 1925 aged 77.

309. In memory of ALEXANDER HAY, Crofter, Orton, who died 9th Novr. 1856, aged 76 years. MARGARET ELLIS, his wife who died 1st June 1852, aged 77 years. Also their son JOHN HAY, Elgin, who died 8th May 1895, aged 81 years. And MARGARET MACINTOSH, his wife who died 24th March 1891, aged 77 years. Erected by ALEXANDER HAY, Surveyor, Edinburgh

(*Mason, W.T. Hendry, Elgin.*)

310.   Erected by ARTHER (*sic*) SINCLAR (*sic*), in memory of his son JAMES, who died at Urquhart, the 18TH February 1870, aged 17 years. And of the said ARTHUR SINCLAIR who died 18TH January 1880, aged 65 years. And his wife MARGARET ROY who died 10TH February 1900 aged 83 years. Also of their son ALEXANDER who died at Threapland, 2ND September 1925, aged 72 years. And his wife JESSIE MUSTARD, who died 24TH Augt. 1930, aged 74 years.
(*Mason, W.T. Hendry, Elgin.*)

311.   Erected by JANET HOOD to the memory of hir (*sic*) beloved husband GEORGE SINCLAR (*sic*), late Merchant in Urquhart, who died March 9th 1847 aged 40 years.

312.   Erected by JAMES YOUNIE, Redburn to the memory of his daughters, ISABELLA, who died at Elgin 20TH May 1870, aged 17 years. HELEN, who died at Redburn 27TH February 1883, aged 37 years. Also his wife, HELEN HOOD, who died at Redburn, 3RD December 1884 aged 74 years. Also of the said JAMES YOUNIE who died 7TH December 1887 aged 77 years.
(*Mason, T. Goodwillie.*)

313.   In loving memory of ALEXANDER FINDLAYSON who died at Meft, Urquhart, on 23RD July 1902, aged 70 years. Also of his son JAMES, who died on 13TH March 1869, aged 2 years. And of his wife JANET INCH, who died 24TH January 1911, aged 82 years.

314.   In loving memory of MARGARET M^{c}INTOSH, beloved wife of JOHN ROSS, who died at Kingston 13. May 1923, aged 75. And their son WILLIAM who fell in action at Arras, 9. April 1917, aged 27. Also the said JOHN ROSS, who died at Garmouth, on 19. May 1937, aged 84. Also their son JAMES, who died 26. Aug. 1960, aged 73.

315.   In memory of our mother BARBARA MACKAY, who died at Longhill Sep^t. 11. 1904.

316.   Erected by CHARLES SMITH, in memory of his beloved wife JESSIE MANN SMITH, who died 6TH Oct. 1921, aged 56 years. The said CHARLES SMITH, who died 20TH Jan. 1925, aged 81 years.
(*Mason, J.S. Morren, South S^t., Elgin.*)

317.   Sacred to the memory of ROBERT T. SMITH, Mains, Urquhart, who died 29TH May 1945, aged 70 years. Also his eldest daughter HELEN, wife of DAVID FORREST who died at Mains, Urquhart, 4TH May 1934, aged 33 years. Also his wife MARGARET FETTES SHAW, who died 4TH May 1946, aged 67 years.

318.   In loving memory of ELIZA MILTON, beloved wife of JOHN FORSYTH, Cowslack, Blackhills, who died 8TH May 1904 aged 42 years. Also the said JOHN FORSYTH, who died 4TH Decr. 1906 aged 58 years. Also of their son,

Gunner JOHN FORSYTH, Royal Garrison Artillery, who was killed in action in France 17TH Aug. 1917 aged 27 years interred at Talana Farm Cemetery, Boesinghe, and their daughter MARGARET who died 16TH Feb. 1966, aged 71 years.
"Blessed are the dead who died in the Lord."

319. In loving memory of ANDREW FORSYTH who died at Stonehouse, 20TH July 1916 aged 76 years. Also his wife ISABELLA HOOD died at Elm Cottage, Lhanbryde, 7TH May 1942 aged 98 years. Also his mother MARGARET TORRIE, who died at Mountswift, 6TH July, 1905 aged 96 years. Also her daughter MARGARET FORSYTH who died at Lhanbryde, 19TH May 1876 aged 31 years. Also his beloved son ALEX^R HOOD FORSYTH who died at Stonehouse, 16TH Nov. 1918 aged 35 years. Deeply regretted. And his daughter MARGARET who died 17TH July 1971 aged 85.
"For our light affliction, which is but for a moment, worketh for us a far more exceeding and eternal weight of glory."

320. In loving memory of JOHN M^{c}INTOSH who died at Newland of Clune, Auldearn 17TH April 1932 aged 81. And his wife ISABELLA JACK died 21ST Jan. 1930 aged 72. Also their son JAMES A. M^{c}INTOSH died 29TH Aug. 1937 aged 39. Erected by their son JAMES.
(Mason, J.R. Henderson, Elgin.)

321. In loving memory of JAMES TAYLOR, Farmer, Darkland, who died at Lhanbryde 3RD March 1949 aged 89 years. Also his wife JANET LESLIE CRUICKSHANK who died at Lhanbryde 3RD August 1951 aged 84 years. Their son JAMES TAYLOR died 23RD Feb. 1979 aged 69 years. And their daughter JANET LESLIE TAYLOR, Nursing Sister at Stracathro, Brechin, died 23RD Nov. 1993 aged 97 years.

322. In loving memory of our dear sons, JAMES CHRISTIE who died 15TH May 1934 aged 6 years. Also ALEXANDER MACKENZIE (ALISTAIR) who died 7TH July 1953 aged 31 years. And my loving husband ERNEST FORDHAM CHRISTIE who died 22ND April 1984 aged 84 years, and his beloved wife CAROLINE M^{c}KENZIE who died 6TH Aug. 1985 aged 85 years.

322a. *Mason's Block.*
C. C.

322b. *Mason's Block.*
E. F. C.

323. In loving memory of my dear husband ROBERT TAYLOR who died at 'Siantar', Lhanbryde, 29TH Jan. 1942 aged 52 years, and his wife JANET BRANDER who died 13TH Jan. 1983 aged 93 years. And son ROBERT ALEXANDER (ADI) who died 26TH Oct. 1999 aged 75 years.

324. Sacred to the memory of DAVID CRUICKSHANK, Farmer, Upper Meft, who died 22ND Dec. 1943 aged 66 years, also his wife HELEN MICHIE who

died at Lhanbryde 21ST May 1962, aged 82 years, also their daughter HELEN MARGARET CRUICKSHANK (ELMA) of Lhanbryde who died 24TH Dec. 2004 aged 81 years. CRUICKSHANK.

325. 1916. Erected by JANE REID, in memory of her beloved husband JAMES MITCHELL DUNCAN, who died at Urquhart 3RD Decr. 1914 aged 87 years. Also her son JOHN, who died at Urquhart 10TH Novr. 1912 aged 51 years. Also her son WILLIAM, who died 23RD Jany. 1867 aged 1 year and 7 months. Also the said JANE REID who died at Urquhart 13TH Decr. 1928 aged 92 years. "Peace perfect peace."
      (*Mason, S.B. Davidson.*)

326. To the memory of WILLIAM PANTON, Newton who died 27 May 1891 and his wife MARY PANTON, who died 5 Feby. 1917, also of their parents ALEXANDER PANTON, Newton, and his wife, also of their grand-parents and great-grand-parents of Hatton, circa. 1710

327. In loving memory of Major GEORGE GRANT PETRIE, T.D. Inchbroom who died 8 April 1956 aged 59 years.

328. *Cross.*
      In memory of ALEXANDER PANTON, Farmer, Newton, who died 9TH September 1881 aged 70 years. Erected by his beloved wife CHARLOTTE MARSHALL, who died 6TH July 1891 aged 59 years. "Blessed are the dead which die in the Lord."

329. Sacred to the memory of ALEXANDER EDDIE, Barmuckity, who departed this life 28th April 1838, aged 82 years. Also JANE ANDERSON, his spouse, who died 26th April 1847, aged 75 years. This stone is erected by their affectionate son JOHN EDDIE. Interred here is the said JOHN EDDIE, who died at Birchfield, 25th March 1869, aged 63 years.

329a. *Flat stone.*
      This stone is erected by IAMES EDIE, Farmer in Mains of Dunkenty & his spouse MARGRET WRIGHT who died in the year 1762 & their son IAMES EDIE who died in the year 1771.
      Whose bodys lys here his goutcher & his grand who lived & died in the Parish of Urquhart on a farm tack of land with other children & neer (*sic*) friends.
      Note: goutcher means grandfather.
      Title 'grand' possibly should have read grandam meaning grandmother. The use of the term goutcher would appear to be fairly uncommon. See personal communication from Mrs Betty Willsher.

329b. Erected … (*h*)er husband …. FORSYTH, Greens of Coxton, ?TH April 1878, aged 43 years. And their daughter JANE, who died 3RD June 1883 aged 21 years. Also JOHN FORSYTH, Farmer, who died at Moss of Barmuckity 16TH June 1917, aged 59 years. Also his wife MARGARET M^{c}ADAM who died at Forres 20TH Feb. 1933 aged 76 years.

330. *Wall plaque.*
Erected by JOHN CRUICKSHANK, in memory of his daughter CHARLOTTE who died 9TH March 1860, aged 13 years, and also of his wife CHARLOTTE BROWN, who died 10TH Decr. 1861, aged 54 years. The said JOHN CRUICKSHANK, died at Barmuckity, 4TH Novr. 1868, aged 55 years. (*Mason, T^{hos}. Goodwillie, Sculp., Elgin.*)

331. *Wall plaque.*
This stone is erected here by THOMAS GILZEAN, Writer in Elgin in memory of ELIZABETH TOD his mother who died 16th December 1781 aged 67 years & GEORGE GILZEAN his father, who died the 31st December 1784 aged 73 & of ALEX^R GILZEAN in Meft, their son who died the 26th Nou^r.(*sic*) 1792 aged 55 & of ISOBEL ROY his spouse who died on the 5th day of Novr. 1814.

332. *Table stone, very worn.*
Sacred to the memory of ALEXANDER BROWN, sometime Farmer, in Upper Meft who died on the 17th April 1842 aged 75? and of ELIZABETH GILZEAN his spouse who died on the 19?th Jan. 1841? aged 78 and also of their youngest son D^r. THOMAS BROWN who died 6th September 1846 at Morant Bay, Jamaica aged 36 years.

333. *Stone marked on 1978 plan but no inscription recorded in 1978 survey, no stone now visible.*

334. In memory of JOHN DEAN, Nether Meft, died 4-4-1921 (*4th April*) aged 78. His wife MARY ANN GORDON, died 19-8-1931 (*19th August*) aged 82. And their family MARY ANN died in infancy. BATHIA died in infancy. JANE ANN died in infancy WILLIAM NORVAL died 17-10-1942 (*17th October*) aged 50.

335. 1853. Erected by WILLIAM MITCHELL in memory of his parents and brother. JAMES MITCHELL who died 12th April 1820 aged 23 years. His wife ANN FINDLAY, who died 31st January 1826 aged 25 years. His mother JEAN DONALDSON who died 18th February 1829 aged 62 years. And his father PETER MITCHELL who died 22nd April 1850 aged 61 years.

335a. *Mason's Block.*
T. D.

336. Erected by JOHN BIRRELL in memory of his beloved wife ELIZABETH PROCTOR who died at Nether Meft 27TH May 1930 aged 78 years. Also in memory of the said JOHN BIRRELL who died at Nether Meft, 9TH December 1936 aged 86 years.
(*Mason, Robertson, Hardgate, Aberdeen.*)

337. Sacred to the memory of MARY GREIG, the beloved wife of JOHN HENDRY who died at Urquhart 30TH Septr. 1896, aged 58 years. Also of the said JOHN HENDRY, who died 1ST July 1913, aged 73 years. Also their elder daughter JANE died 3RD Octr. 1932. Interred in Borthwick Churchyard.

338. In loving memory of ALEXANDER DEAN, Farmer who died at Jointurelands 9TH June 1917 aged 60 years. Also his son ALEXANDER JAMIESON who fell in action in the Third Battle of Ypres, Belgium, 31ST July 1917 aged 26 years. Also his son WILLIAM DUNCAN, who died in infancy. And JESSIE TAYLOR his wife, who died 2ND June 1954 aged 87 years. Also their daughter JESSIE TAYLOR DEAN who died in Aberdeen 20TH Feb. 1971 aged 73 years. And their sons, GEORGE HUGH GRANT who died at Jointurelands 26TH Aug. 1975 aged 66 years, and WILLIAM SYMON, Farmer, who died at Elgin 23RD April 1976 aged 76 years. DEAN.

339. Erected by JAMES DEAN, Farmer, Jointer, in memory of his father JAMES DEAN who died 13TH Decr. 1871, aged 78 years. And his mother JANET YOUNG who died 4TH Feby. 1879, aged 93 years.

340. 1881. Erected by BATHIA SANDISON in memory of her beloved husband JAMES DEAN, Farmer, Jointure, Leuchars, who died 1ST July 1880, aged 63 years, and the said BATHIA SANDISON, who died at Jointure, Leuchars, 9TH June 1884, aged 60 years.
(Mason, W.T. Hendry, Abbey Street, Elgin.)

340a. *Mason's Block.*
J. D.

341. In loving memory of DUNCAN MACKENZIE, Cappies Hill, who entered into rest 27TH Septr 1900 aged 70 years. A just man made perfect, & his son WILLIAM JAMES, who died at Suison, California, 19TH Jany. 1891 aged 27 years. Also his daughter ELLEN who died 1ST Feby. 1860 aged 10 months. Also of ANN PIRIE wife of the above DUNCAN MACKENZIE who died at Cappies Hill 20TH Jany. 1902 aged 71 years. Also his son GEORGE ALEXANDER MACKENZIE who died at Aberdeen 13TH Jany. 1905 aged 49 years.

342. 1895. In memory of ALEXANDER WEBSTER, Farmer, Lochs, who died there 6TH Octr. 1893 in his 74TH year. And of his wife MARGARET CUMMING, who died at Garmouth 24TH June 1899 in her 79TH year. Also of his daughters MARY, & BARBARA, who died in infancy. And MARGARET, wife of JAMES GAY, New Brompton, Kent, who died there 25TH Octr. 1891, aged 41 years. Interred in Gillingham Cemetery. Also of his father GEORGE WEBSTER, Farmer, Lochs, who died there 25TH Feby. 1885, in his 92ND year, and his mother ISOBELLE PHIMISTER, died at Lochs, 14TH Decr. 1879.

342a. *Mason's Block.*
W. R.

343. Erected by HELEN SHIACH in loving memory of her husband JOHN SHIACH who died at Burnside Cottage, Lhanbryde, 18TH May 1924 aged 80 years, and of his wife HELEN M^cINTYRE who died 16TH Feb. 1928 aged 86 years.

344. Erected by ALEXANDER SHIACH in loving memory of his wife HELLEN SIMPSON who died at Greens of Coxton, on the 14TH day of February 1835/6? aged 35/85? years.

344a. *Mason's Block.*
W. R.

345. Erected by GEORGE GERRIE, Mason, Elgin, in memory of his wife MARGARET ROSS, who died at Elgin 24TH November 1868 aged 37 years, and their children JAMES, and JOHN, who died in infancy. Also his second wife JANE CUMMING, who died at New-Elgin 3RD July 1876, aged 35 years. And their daughter JANE ANN who died in infancy. Also WILLIAM A. GERRIE who died 18TH May 1889, aged 19 years, and of the said GEORGE GERRIE who died at Nicol Street, New-Elgin 15TH January 1893, aged 63 years.

345a. *Mason's Block.*
C. S.

346. Erected by JAMES ROSS, Farmer, Bailies-lands, Leuchars, to the memory of his beloved wife ELSPET GERRIE, who departed this life on the 6th of August 1854. Also the said JAMES ROSS who died 15th January 1874 aged 72 years. And of his daughter HELEN, who died 19th May 1894 aged 73 years.

347. Sacred to the memory of WILLIAM ROSS, Farmer, Leuchars, who died the 25th November 1864 aged 84 years. Also his spouse CHRISTINA ROSS or MILNE, who died the 29th August 1850 aged 70 years. Also their daughters, ISABELLA who died at Leuchars, the 7th October 1895 aged 87 years. And ELIZABETH who died at Aberdeen, the 10th February 1899 aged 80 years. And who is also interred here.

347a. *Mason's Block.*
W. ROSS, Leuchars.

347b. *Mason's Block.*
A. F.

348. To the memory of WILLIAM FORSYTH, late Gardner (*sic*) to PATRICK WILLIAMS Esqr. Temple House, Berks., son of JOHN FORSYTH, late Farmer, Luchars (*sic*), who died Novr. 13th 1844 aged 44 years. Erected by his sisters MARGRET & EUPHEMIA, and his son WILLIAM.

349. Erected in memory of MARGARET SIMPSON, relict of JOHN FORSYTH, sometime Farmer in Leuchars, who died 24th March 1835 aged 81 years, and of JOHN FORSYTH, son of the above, who died 18TH July 1844, aged 52. Also his wife ANNIE BROWN who died 4TH Jany. 1879, aged 81. And their family, JOHN, ISABELLA, EUPHEMIA & MARGARET.

350. Erected in memory of JAMES SINCLAIR, who died at Urquhart 21th (sic) day of May 1845 aged 80 yers (sic). His wife ANN GRAY, died 2nd Feby. 1851 aged 80 years.

351. Erected by MARGARET ROBERTSON and family in loving memory of her husband JOHN SINCLAIR, who died at Lhanbryde 18TH May 1913 aged 63 years. And of the said MARGARET ROBERTSON, who died at Elgin 1ST June 1952, aged 94 years. Interred in Elgin Cemetery. "He shall cover thee with his feathers and under his wings shalt thou trust." Psalms 91 Ver. 4

352. Erected by JAMES HENDRY, Edinburgh, in memory of his father, JOHN HENDRY, Urquhart, who died 13TH June 1887, aged 76 years. Also in memory of his sister JANE, beloved wife of DAVID HENRY, (sic) who died suddenly at Craigesk 18TH March 1888, aged 43 years and is interred in Newbattle Churchyard. And of his mother SARAH HENDRY, who died 1ST March 1893, aged 77 years.

353. Sacred to the memory of GEORGE YOUNG who died at Urquhart in September 1828 aged 2 years. ALEXANDER YOUNG who died at Urquhart in February 1832 aged 22 years. JEAN YOUNG who died at Urquhart in October 1837 aged 24 years. And ISABELLA YOUNG who died at Urquhart in September 1842 aged 25 years. The beloved children of WILLIAM YOUNG & JEAN BREMNER. Also the said WILLIAM YOUNG who died at Urquhart on 23rd March 1864 aged 87 years.
JANE BREMNER widow of the said WILLIAM YOUNG died 20TH Novr. 1878 aged 90 years. Also ELEZABETH (sic) YOUNG died 28TH May 1904 aged 85 years.

354. Sacred to the memory of MARY RENNIE, the beloved wife of JOHN YOUNG, who died at Urquhart 5TH January 1893, aged 66 years. Also their son JOHN, who died in infancy. And the said JOHN YOUNG, who died at Urquhart 7TH May 1902 aged 73 years. Also his son JOHN, who died at Gray's Hospital, Elgin 16TH November 1913 aged 48 years.

355. 1895. In loving memory of JAMES WRIGHT, who died at Tiendland, 12TH Sep^t. 1890 aged 73 years. Also four children who died in infancy. Also his wife MARY DUNCAN who died 22ND August 1904 aged 78 years. Their grandson JAMES WRIGHT son of M^{RS}. MACKINTOSH who died 26TH February 1934 aged 51 years. The said M^{RS}. MACKINTOSH who died 25TH December 1936 aged 75 years. Her daughters, JESSIE died 16TH March 1956. LIZZIE died 14TH March 1972. MARY died 23RD July 1975. And her son GEORGE died Edmonton, Canada, 15TH Dec. 1968.
(Mason, W.T. Hendry, Elgin.)

356. In memory of MARGARET ROBERTSON wife of JAMES DUNCAN, Farmer, Kempstown, who died there 5th April 1827, aged 35 years. Also the above JAMES DUNCAN who died at Keith 10th May 1869 aged 87 years.

357. Be ye also ready. Erected by WILLIAM ROSS, Meft, in loving memory of his family, WILLIAM ALEXANDER ROSS, Brakesman, G.N.S.R., who

met his death by accident at Aberdeen Station on the 3RD day of February 1897, aged 22 years. Also MARGARET ROSS who died 21ST February 1883, aged 16 years. Also WILLIAM and JESSIE who died in infancy. Also of his wife MARGARET BARRON who died 17TH October 1907 aged 69 years. And of the said WILLIAM ROSS, who died 22ND July 1911, aged 70 years. Also JESSIE ROSS, niece of the said WM. ROSS, died in Edinburgh, 10TH June 1946, aged 82 years.
(Mason, W.T. Hendry, Elgin.)

357a. *Mason's Block.*
W. A. R.

358. *Broken stone.*
1891.   Erected by WILLIAM ROSS, Meft, in memory of his father WILLIAM ROSS, who died 9TH Jany. 1891 aged 84 years. And his mother HELEN SIMPSON who died 6TH Jany.1891, aged 84

358a. *Mason's Block.*
W. R.

359. In loving memory of my dear brother WILLIAM HENDERSON died 24TH May 1971 aged 56.

360. In loving memory of our dear mother, ELIZABETH MATTHEW died 10TH June 1935 aged 46. Our dear father, GORDON THOMSON died 2ND Jan. 1970 aged 72.

361. In memory of JAMES BELL, who died at Forres 19TH May 1883, aged 58 years. Also in loving remembrance of CATHERINE BELL, wife of ALEXANDER ASHER who died at Moss of Barmuckity 11TH September 1915 aged 80 years. Also the said ALEXANDER ASHER who died 17TH August 1918 aged 87 years. And his son ALEXANDER ASHER who died at Moss of Barmuckity 15TH January 1940. Also his wife HELEN LAWSON who died 21ST January 1931. This stone is placed here by his sisters.
(Mason.,W.T. Hendry, Abbey St., Elgin.)

361a. *Mason's Block.*
A. A.

362. *Obelisk.*
East face.
Sacred to the memory of GORDON BRANDER, who died at Bogside, Nairn 17TH Sep. 1904, aged 82 years. Also JANE MILNE, his wife who died at Oruba Villa, Forres, 24TH Feb. 1911, aged 76 years. JANE, daughter of the above, died at Elgin, 25TH Dec. 1941 aged 86.
South face.
Also in memory of ALEXANDER BRANDER, Nether Meft, who died 24TH March 1890, aged 94 years. Also ANN BRANDER his wife, who died Sep. 1839, aged 30 years. Also his sisters MARGARET, who died 30TH March

1855, aged 73 years. HELEN, who died 26TH May 1894, aged 94 years. Their daughter ANNE BRANDER, who died 13TH March 1932, aged 93 years.
North face.
Also in memory of JAMES BRANDER, Greens of Meft, who died 28TH Feb. 1866, aged 77 years. Also JESSIE M[c]KENZIE his wife, who died 12TH Sep. 1868, aged 76 years. Also ELIZABETH their daughter, who died 24TH Oct. 1899 aged 77 years.
(Mason, Henderson, Forres.)

363.   *Flat stone.*
This stone is placed here by IOHN BRANDER, Farmer in Unthank. In memory of my grandfather IOHN BRANDER who lived a portioner in Urquhart who died 1712 & my father IAMES BRANDER who died in Unthank August 1727.

364.   *Flat stone.*
Here lyes the body of IAMES CHALMERS sometime Farmer in Lewchars (*sic*), who died Ian[r]. the 18th 1741 & his spouse MARGRET DUNCAN who died March the 9th 1717 & ISOBEL[L] (*sic*) FIMISTER his spouse, in his second marriage, who died the (*blank*) day of (*blank*) 17(*blank*) & their son IOHN CHALMERS who died the 6th day of Feb[r]. 1747.

365.   *Possible base with Mason's name Camero(n)*

366.   Erected to the memory of JOHN ARCHIBALD by his beloved wife and family who died at Lochs of Urquhart, 12TH August 1862 aged 47 years. Also of their daughter MARY who died 14TH May 1858 aged 15 years. And of MARGARET DUNCAN, wife of the said JOHN ARCHIBALD who died at Lochs of Urquhart 6TH February 1896 aged 76 years.

367.   In loving memory of WILLIAM SIMPSON died 5TH Oct. 1920. Also his wife JESSIE ANDERSON died 5TH April 1937. Their daughters, CAROLINE JESSIE died in infancy. CHRISTINA MARY died 6TH April 1943. JESSIE DUFF SIMPSON died 11TH Feb. 1953.

368.   Erected by JANET ROBSON, in memory of her husband ALEXANDER SIMPSON who died at Slentack, 26TH April 1876, aged 56 years and of their daughter, ANNIE who died 1856, aged 6 months. Also of their son, ALEXANDER SIMPSON, who died at Slentack, 27TH April 1883, aged 18 years. JANET ROBSON died 13TH July 1901. Also their daughter JANE SIMPSON who died at Perth, 6th February 1934, aged 74 years.
Name Janet has been re-carved and corrected by the mason.
(Mason, T. Goodwillie.)

369.   In loving memory of JOAN SIMPSON who died 1913 aged 52. Also her husband JOHN FORSYTH who died at Boharm 1923.

370.   Erected by the friends, in memory of JOHN SIMPSON, Farmer, Coats of Innes, & Feuer, Lossiemouth, who died 23RD March 1860, aged 75 years, also his sister, ANN, who died 6TH January 1865, aged 75.

(*Mason, Goodwillie.*)

371. In memory of JOHN FRENCH, Hamlets, Drainie, died 10TH June 1935 aged 84 yrs. His wife MARY MANN died 3RD March 1919 aged 70 yrs. His mother ISABELLA FRENCH died 26TH April 1900 aged 70 yrs.

371a. *Heart shaped plaque.*
FRENCH. In memory of my Father and Mother, from BELLA.

372. To the memory of JAMES LAMB, late farmer in Nether Eassel (*sic*)who died the 20 August 1834 aged 50 years. Erected by JANE PATERSON his spouse who died 7th Feby. 1854 aged 72 years. And HUGH LAMB their son who died the 16 August 1834 aged 4 years. Their son WILLIAM died 13th April 1855, aged 29 years. And JOHN died 1st April 1871 aged 60 years.

373. In loving memory of our daughter BETTY FORSYTH who died 1ST Feb. 1935 aged 15 years and of ALEXANDER FORSYTH who died at Innesmill 21ST Oct. 1942 aged 71 years and his wife ANN M^{C}PHERSON who died at Bishopmill 9TH Dec. 1945 aged 70 years.

374. In loving memory of CHRISTINA A. M^{c}ARTHUR who died 1ST Jan. 1944 aged 55 years. Also her husband JAMES MORRISON who died 7TH May 1962 aged 71 years. Their son JOHN (IAN) who died 5TH Feb. 2002 aged 76 years.

374a. *Heart shaped plaque.*
In memory of SAMUEL ALEXANDER, died 26. Aug. 1882 aged 69. His wife HELLEN MURRAY died 22. Sep. 1898 aged 85 and my sister BETSY died in infancy. H. SIM.

375. In memory of our dear brother PETER M^{c}PHERSON who died at Lochhill Cottages 1ST August 1941 aged 62 years. At rest.

376. In loving memory of JAMES MILNE, Farmer, Kennieshillock, beloved husband of ISABELLA BRANDER who died 12TH March 1945 aged 72 years. Also the said ISABELLA BRANDER who died 20TH Nov. 1965 aged 85 years.

Information from Antiquarian and other published sources.

Di Folco. J. PSAS 1966-1967

A small Calvary Cross slab 25 inches by 11 inches, with dog-tooth ornamentation round its edges, the body of the slab contains an incised Calvary Cross with a nimbus and radiating bands of light from the shaft which is mounted on two steps. There are traces of incised marks to the dexter of the cross.

This is the stone which was rescued from the ruins of Urquhart Priory.

Index of names in the Old Churchyard of Urquhart

URQUHART OLD CHURCHYARD . MORAY

MBGRG   BBB 11/7/05   NOT TO SCALE

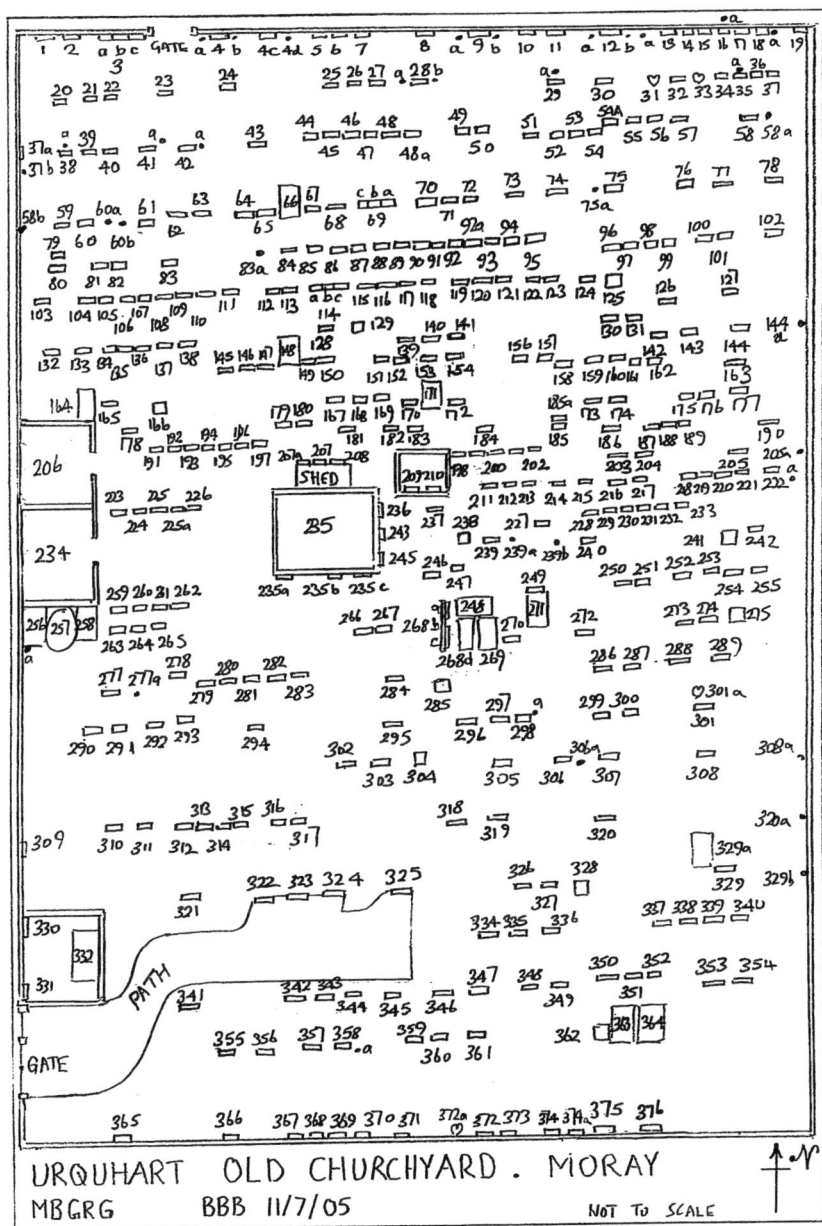

Plan of the Old Churchyard of Urquhart